Where **Growth Mindset,**
Habits of Mind
and Practice ***Unite***

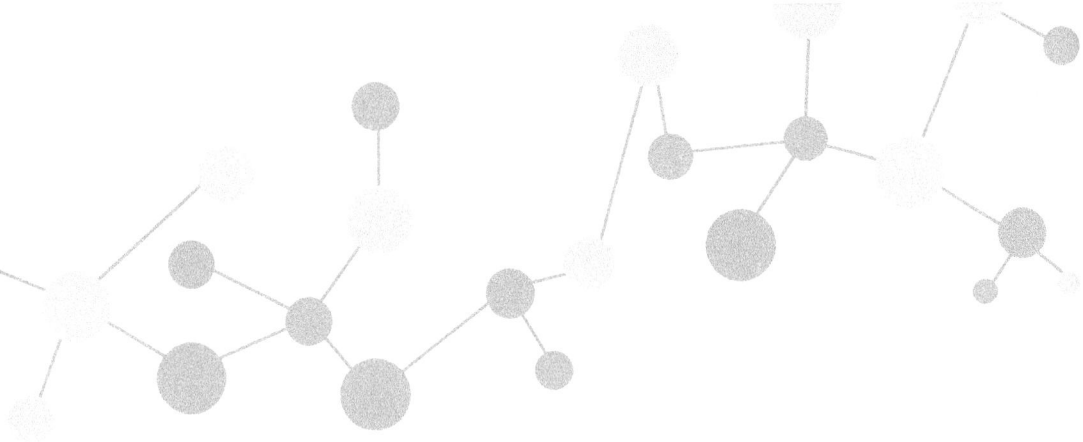

THE AGILE LEARNER

JAMES ANDERSON

First published in 2017 by Hawker Brownlow
This edition published in 2023 by James Anderson

© James Anderson 2023
The moral rights of the author have been asserted

All rights reserved. Except as permitted under the *Australian Copyright Act 1968* (for example, a fair dealing for the purposes of study, research, criticism or review), no part of this book may be reproduced, stored in a retrieval system, communicated or transmitted in any form or by any means without prior written permission.

All inquiries should be made to the author.

ISBN: 978-0-6459129-1-3

Cover photo credit: Fiona Basile
Cover art designed by Harryarts/Freepik

Disclaimer
The material in this publication is of the nature of general comment only, and does not represent professional advice. It is not intended to provide specific guidance for particular circumstances and it should not be relied on as the basis for any decision to take action or not take action on any matter which it covers. Readers should obtain professional advice where appropriate, before making any such decision. To the maximum extent permitted by law, the author and publisher disclaim all responsibility and liability to any person, arising directly or indirectly from any person taking or not taking action based on the information in this publication.

Contents

About the Author v

Endorsements ix

Downloadable Teacher Resources xi

Acknowledgements xiii

Section 1: The Agile Learner 1

Section 2: Mindsets 19
2.1 Why Mindset Is Important 21
2.2 The Mindset Continuum and Mindset Movers 35
2.3 Teacher Mindset 45

Section 3: How Do We Achieve Growth? 57
3.1 The Rule of Choice 63
3.2 The Rule of Practice 75
3.3 The Rule of Effort 109
3.4 The Rule of Unlimited Growth 137

Section 4: New Ideas About Talent 147

Suggested Readings 167

About the Author

James first became interested in how to teach students to become better thinkers as a classroom teacher in the late 90s. Later, as a school leader, he spearheaded a national research project focused on infusing Art Costa and Bena Kallick's Habits of Mind into schools and classrooms.

The key finding of this project was that the Habits of Mind were only part of the solution. To see improvements in student learning outcomes, James discovered it was crucial to accompany the Habits of Mind with the development of a Growth Mindset.

James is now passionate about supporting schools and teachers to enable students to thrive in a rapidly changing, increasingly complex and highly challenging world. His learning has taken him beyond thinking skills and Mindsets to the concept of the Agile Learner – someone who not only understands they are capable of learning to behave more intelligently, but who knows how to go about achieving it!

The foundation of James's work is the Growth Mindset. James takes teachers beyond simple social media catchphrases to create a teaching framework that develops robust and enduring Growth Mindsets in the classroom. By challenging teachers' own Mindsets, he equips them to nurture Growth Mindsets in their students.

James skilfully unites the Habits of Mind, Anders Ericsson's critical work on practice and Carol Dweck's work on Growth Mindset. In doing so, he creates a powerful combination that increases student efficacy and achieves greater learning outcomes through the development of Learning Agility.

James believes it will be *human* intelligence that will be the most valuable commodity in the future. Futurists predict a world that will be dominated by *artificial* intelligence – machines that will do our high-level thinking for us. But it's not computers we need to develop; it's the minds of our children. James gives teachers the pedagogy that enables their students to develop their human intelligence.

Having worked in classrooms and with schools for more than two decades, James knows that the students of today face problems fundamentally different to those of the past. Problems such as climate change, population growth and the depletion of natural resources are more global in their scope, more severe in their consequences, and more immediate in their nature. James firmly believes solving these problems requires today's students to become smarter than the students of the past.

We don't just need better thinkers – we need more *agile* thinkers. We need to teach students what to do when they don't know what to do. We need to help them recognise that they can't solve the problems they face with their existing skills and abilities. And we need to ensure they know *how* to improve their skills and abilities through Learning Agility. In doing so, we increase human intelligence. James shows you how to do this!

James Anderson regularly speaks at conferences around Australia and overseas. He is a Certified Speaking Professional (CSP). As an author, he has published *Succeeding with Habits of Mind* and *The Agile Learner*, as well as numerous e-books. He has published with Art Costa and Bena Kallick in *Learning and Leading with Habits of Mind* and *Habits of Mind*

About the Author

Across the Curriculum. His regular blogs are also read by thousands of educators around the world. James is certified by Mindset Works as a Growth Mindset trainer and is an affiliate director of the Institute for Habits of Mind. You can find out more about James and the services he offers at www.jamesanderson.com.au

Endorsements

The Agile Learner synthesizes three important theories of learning: Dweck's work on Mindsets, Ericsson's work on developing highly skilled performances, and our work on Habits of Mind. Anderson weaves these three together to create a rich tapestry of possibilities for opening the power and potential for all of our students as we do away with the myths that limit learners and open the door for unlimited learning. This book would be a terrific book study for groups of teachers as they study the theories and examples in the book and examine their practices.

Art Costa and Bena Kallick, co-authors of Habits of Mind

Over the last decade, there has been an explosion in the number of professional development providers offering their services in Australia. James Anderson is a member of an elite group of Australian trainers who consistently provide practical, high quality and thought-provoking support to educators as they seek to improve their practice.

James Anderson is routinely ahead of the educational curve in his research and workshop offerings. He was one of the first to provide consistent and practical support for schools using the Habits of Mind. He also introduced teachers to the principles of Dweck's Growth Mindset work years before it became widely known.

James presents complex ideas and theories from a wide range of complementary educational researchers in a way that inspires and supports excellence in teacher practice. In workshops, James helps teachers to create a system of robust and deliverable instructional methods built on current research findings from the fields of education, brain science, psychology and business. His sessions are thought-provoking, and though they sometimes challenge our assumptions, are always engaging and fun.

James' new book is an absolute gift to educators looking to understand and utilise the powerful principles of Growth Mindset approaches. The book provides guidance and clarity, while avoiding the hype that has come about by the oft-times uninformed marketing of 'Growth Mindset' in the form of superficial training sessions, books and the indiscriminate coining of Mindset sayings in conferences and social media.

While honouring Costa and Kallick's related work on the development of productive Habits of Mind, James explores both the core principles of Dweck's Mindsets and her later work. A significant account of Dweck's recent critical re-evaluation of some of her initial suggested practices is informative.

Alex Delaforce Med., Head of Teaching and Learning Processes,
Coomera Anglican College

Downloadable Teacher Resources

James Anderson has created a number of infographics to support the ideas explained in *The Agile Learner*.

These include:
- The Mindset Continuum
- Understanding the Fixed and Growth Mindset Responses
- The Learning Plateau
- The Emotional Cascade of the Performance Plateau
- 16 Habits of Mind
- Learning Agility
- Effective Effort Matrix

All of these infographic are available in large format PDFs as free downloads from:

www.jamesanderson.com.au/p/TheAgileLearnerDownloads/

You are welcome to reproduce these infographics in your school, and to share them with the educational community.

Permission is required before publication in any print media (e.g. books or journals), or in any format where a fee is charged (including course notes where a fee is charged for the course). Copyright for all images remains with James Anderson.

Acknowledgements

I am extremely grateful to the groups and individuals that have helped to shape this book.

Firstly, to the giants whose thoughts and research I have built upon: Professor Carol Dweck, whose work on Mindsets has become the foundation of Learning Agility; Professor Anders Ericsson, who so skilfully outlined the process for acquiring excellence – more educators need to know about this work; and to Professor Art Costa and Dr Bena Kallick, for describing the Habits of Mind and helping to make the world a more thought-filled place.

I must give special thanks to Professor Art Costa and Dr Bena Kallick, not just for their thoughts and research, but also for their active support of my work over many years. You have both been wonderful mentors to me.

There have been so many other people that have played important roles in supporting, challenging and guiding me over the years that there are simply too many to mention here. But you know who you are, and I am grateful to each and every one of you. Without you I would not have been where I am today and able to bring these ideas to the educational community.

Special thanks must also go to my family, Fiona and Lucy, for their constant love and support.

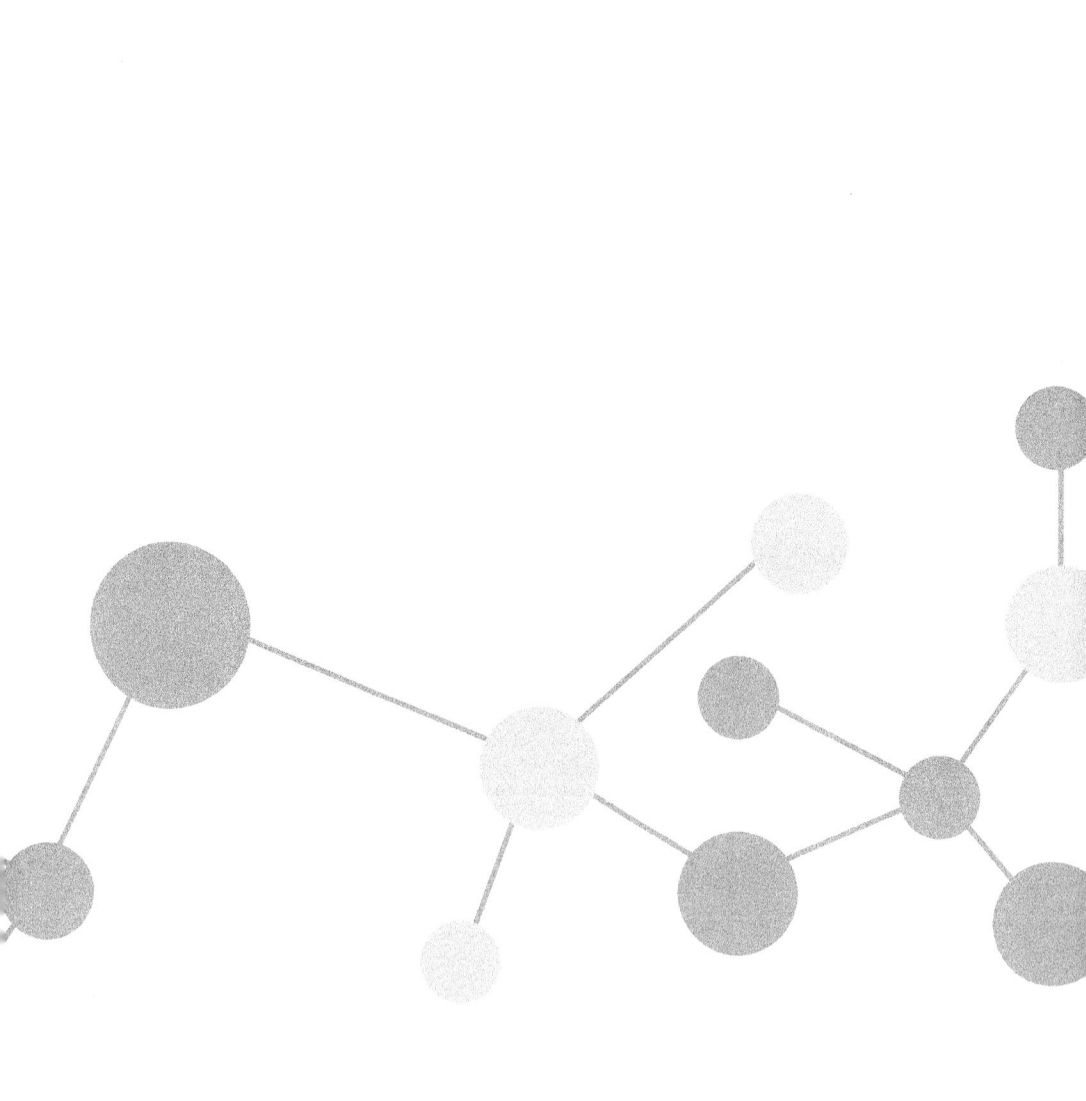

SECTION 1
The Agile Learner

SECTION 1
The Agile Learner

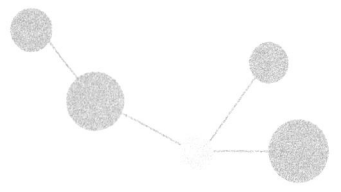

Change and the 21st-Century Learner

You don't have to go far today before someone starts talking to you about the need to prepare our children for the future. Children in our schools will change not only jobs, but careers, multiple times. They will be using technologies that haven't been invented to solve problems that don't yet exist.

Exactly what that future will look like is anyone's guess. Predicting the future is notoriously difficult, and all we can really be sure of is that the world is changing more rapidly now than at any other time in the past. The world is becoming more complex, more uncertain and more changeable than it has ever been before.

In the business world, people talk about these changes as "disruptions": problems that interrupt the current way of working. Today, it's business as usual: systems are in place, people know their roles and all is going well. But then something happens: a new technology emerges, a start-up company doesn't play by "the rules", the political climate changes. Put simply, something occurs that was not expected and, as a result, the business becomes unstable and must either adapt or perish.

In response to these disruptions, many businesses have adopted "agile systems": systems that are responsive and flexible, so that the business can respond to disruptions as they arise. The hope is that if the business is agile enough, it can respond quickly enough to take advantage of opportunities, deal with threats and, ultimately, become more successful. Basically, businesses are trying to ensure that they are increasingly responsive and adaptable in what has become an increasingly changing and challenging environment.

Of course, as educators, it is our job to prepare our young people for this world – a world of change and disruption – and we have been grappling with this challenge for some time. We are aware of the need to develop "21st-century learners", and we know that it is no longer enough to teach children what they need to know for life in a predictable world.

> So, preparing students for a world of change and disruption means we must teach them what to do when they don't know what to do.

In response to this, there has been a shift away from teaching the "hard facts" to teaching the "soft skills". Rather than teaching children what to think, we have been asked to teach students *how* to think. This is not at the expense of content. Rather, we use the content in ways that provide opportunities to help students become better thinkers. The theory is that if we can teach students to be better thinkers, they will be able to respond to challenges and thrive in the 21st century.

There have been many attempts to identify which skills an "effective thinker" possesses. In terms of teaching creativity, Edward de Bono has done great work. The Visible Thinking learning routines from Harvard University likewise provide a set of specific skills that are very useful. David Hyerle and others have produced graphic organisers to help structure student thinking. And there have been many more skills, tools and strategies described that aim to help students become better thinkers.

In my view, the strongest and most complete description of the thinking necessary to succeed in the 21st century is Art Costa and Bena Kallick's Habits of Mind (2008). These sixteen Habits of Mind are the dispositions Costa and Kallick identified as being skilfully and mindfully employed by characteristically successful people when they encounter challenges or disruptions. They are the way successful people behave when the solution to a problem is not immediately apparent. The Habits of Mind capture many of the thinking skills described above, but take them beyond discrete tools to wider-ranging behaviours and dispositions.

However, in my opinion our attempts to teach students "thinking skills" have not been as successful as we had hoped they might be. It is not that these skills aren't necessary – they are. Nor is it that they have been poorly defined. It is simply that being a skilful thinker, although essential, isn't enough to thrive in the 21st century. Also, even though we tried to teach these thinking skills, many students weren't becoming the skilful thinkers we had hoped they would become simply by being taught thinking skills.

An important insight into this problem was provided by Professor Carol Dweck, through her work on Mindsets. In an elegant experiment, Dweck (2006) showed that teaching "study skills" to students had the greatest impact *after* they were first taught about the brain's plasticity. Teaching students how their brain changed in response to learning contributed to the development of a Growth Mindset – an understanding that you can change your most basic characteristics including your talents, intelligence and abilities.

> Part of the reason why the thinking skills movement failed to live up to expectations was because we hadn't first considered the importance of developing a Growth Mindset in our students.

Some students simply weren't getting as much out of our efforts to teach them thinking skills because they had a relatively fixed view of their intelligence and abilities.

Had the importance of Dweck's work come to light before Costa and Kallick published their Habits of Mind, we may well be in a different situation than we are today. But that is not the case, and so we must move forward understanding that developing a Growth Mindset is fundamental to any attempt to teach students to be better thinkers.

Combining a Growth Mindset with the Habits of Mind is a potent combination. Dweck's work highlights the importance of understanding that we are *capable* of developing our most basic characteristics such as our intelligence. Costa and Kallick describe the behaviours and dispositions students must develop in order to actually achieve this more intelligent behaviour. As students apply their Greatness Gap to the Habits of Mind they learn how to behave more intelligently. This results in the development of Learning Power – a capacity to succeed at increasingly difficult tasks.

If the 21st century was simply throwing up more difficult problems for the next generation to solve, developing Learning Power might be enough, but it's not that straightforward. The issue for the next generation is not simply that the problems they face are more difficult, it is that they are occurring in an unpredictable, changing and often volatile environment. We don't just need people who can solve more difficult problems; we need learners who can respond to new, novel problems in a disruptive world. We don't just need powerful thinkers, we need agile ones.

This is where the critical work of Anders Ericsson (1996) comes into play. Ericsson is a world leader in the field of Acquisition of Excellence, and has spent his career describing the process by which peak performers acquire and develop their talents. In short, Ericsson describes the best way to *practice* to increase talents and abilities.

In his most recent book, *Peak: Secrets from the New Science of Expertise* (Houghton Mifflin Harcourt, 2016), Ericsson documents several decades worth of research that captures the essence of the process required to respond effectively when encountering a disruption or challenge. Drawing on wider-ranging studies from doctors to fighter pilots, chess players to classical violin players, he demonstrates the common type of practice top performers engage in as they increase their talents and abilities. This sort of practice involves extending yourself just beyond your "Comfort Zone" into your "Learning Zone". Perhaps most importantly, as we will explore later in this book, this sort of practice results in building new abilities by changing the way your brain is wired.

Ericsson describes this practice as Deliberate or Purposeful Practice. This does not mean we are deliberately practicing – although we are. It means we are deliberately, or purposefully, practicing in a way that is specifically designed to extend our abilities. Unfortunately, many people do not practice this way, and as a result do not extend their abilities. Throughout this book, I refer to Deliberate and Purposeful Practice together as Virtuous Practice, as they have the virtue of leading to further growth.

> The most successful people in the 21st century will be those who are the most responsive: the ones who can adapt in the face of disruption. These people will be able to constantly build new skills and abilities in the face of change.

That is what this book is about: how we, as educators, develop in our students the capacity to become *increasingly effective learners* in a world that is consistently disrupted. For success in the 21st century, we can't just build agile workplaces, we must build Agile Learners.

To develop Agile Learners, we need to bring together the three powerful and complementary understandings that I have introduced above:

1. Professor Carol Dweck's work on Growth Mindset.
2. Professor Art Costa and Dr Bena Kallick's work on the Habits of Mind.
3. Professor Anders Ericsson's work on practice.

The Agile Learner

Graphically, our concept of Learning Agility looks like this:

LEARNING AGILITY

- Mature Habits of Mind
- Build Efficacy
- Virtuous Practice
- Build Power
- Increasing **LEARNING AGILITY**
- Build Potential
- Growth Mindset

None of the three elements on their own is enough. It is not until we combine Mindset with Habits of Mind and Practice that we develop the Agile Learner.

The Agile Learner is someone who recognises that they live in an unpredictable, changeable and disruptive world. The Agile Learner understands that because of this, they can't and don't currently have the capacity to solve every problem they are likely to encounter. Their education has neither equipped them with all the answers, nor the full set of skills they need in order to thrive in the 21st century.

However, the Agile Learner understands that they are capable of changing themselves. They understand that they can develop their Habits of Mind and learn to behave more intelligently. This allows them to engage more effectively in Virtuous Practice and, in doing so, successfully address increasingly difficult problems.

The remainder of this book will unpack what it means to develop Agile Learners, but before we do this, we need to explore one of the experiences many people have when trying to learn something new: the Performance Plateau.

The Performance Plateau

For many people, learning looks like this: they start learning something new and find that progress initially comes easily. New things aren't always hard. We find the right entry point, and our standards improve quickly.

Take, for example, my own experience learning to play golf. I had seen the game played often enough, so I had a vague idea of what was required. I had also played other sports, so I wasn't entirely uncoordinated. I then got a few pointers from friends and went out to play a game of golf. It wasn't a great game, but I managed to hit the ball most of the time.

Occasionally I hit it straight-ish and, when I eventually got to the green, I could tap it around until it fell into the hole. In an effort to improve, I started playing more. I got a few professional lessons, and eliminated the worst of my errors. I improved, for a while. Then the rate of improvement started to decline. I kept playing. I kept doing what I called practice, but I didn't see much improvement. I eventually got to the point where I could accurately tell you how many strokes it was going to take for me to get around the course, give or take a few, but couldn't seem to reduce that number. I'd reached my Performance Plateau.

For many people, the Performance Plateau marks the limit of their abilities; the point at which they have discovered how good they are at something. In terms of golf, something I'm not interested in getting much better at, that's not a problem. I don't play golf to be good at it, I play it to spend an afternoon with mates. It's the 19th hole that's my favourite.

But what if you do want to get better at something? What if you hit the Performance Plateau and can't get any better at something that's important to you? What if it was your job? What if you wanted to solve a problem in your relationship? The Performance Plateau becomes a real problem.

Consider the emotional response to the Performance Plateau for something you want or need to get better at. The early progress is fine, but when things slow down we experience a cascade of emotions. We might feel frustration, as something that was initially easy becomes hard. We struggle as we try to progress and see little result, despite increasing the time and energy we put into the task. Eventually, we experience feelings of failure, then the resignation that this just isn't "us". It's not something we can do, not something we're cut out for.

If we are then placed in a situation where we are asked to do this thing we've found difficult, this thing we "know" we can't do, our feelings might turn to fear. Fear of being put in a position where we know we'll fail. Fear of having our limitations laid bare for the world to see. As a result, we avoid these situations.

Section 1: The Agile Learner

THE NEGATIVE EMOTIONAL CASCADE OF THE PERFORMANCE PLATEAU

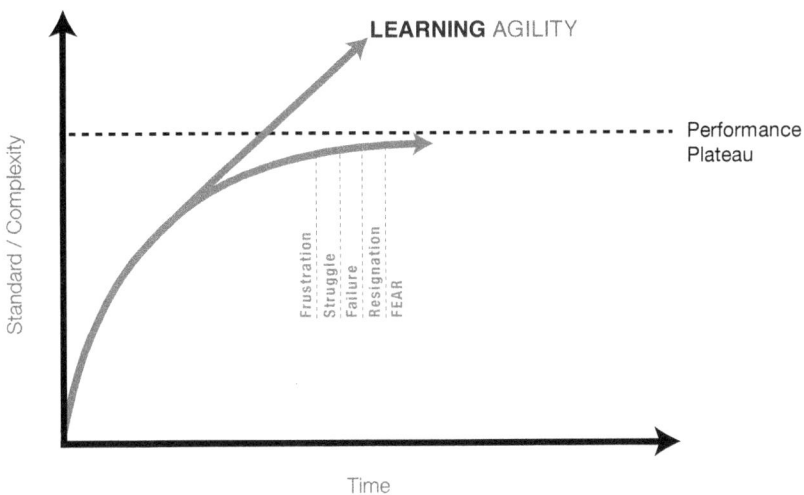

When we experience the Performance Plateau frequently enough, we come to believe that it is the reality of our life. That there are limits to our abilities.

Those limits might be higher in some areas than others, but there is always a limit. More importantly, people have different limits. Some people appear to have their learning plateau set higher than others. What I might find hard, another person finds easy.

Someone with Learning Agility doesn't experience the Performance Plateau. They understand that while the early phase of learning something new might be easy, eventually progress will become difficult. At that point, they must then develop the abilities and engage in the process that will allow them to grow and succeed. Any limit they encounter is temporary.

The cascade of feelings someone with Learning Agility experiences is different to other people. As they work not only on what they are trying to learn, but how they learn, they begin to see progress. Progress gives rise to a feeling of satisfaction and, eventually, achievement, as they accomplish the goals they set for themselves. As more goals are reached, someone with Learning Agility builds confidence, and that confidence leads to the courage to take on new challenges.

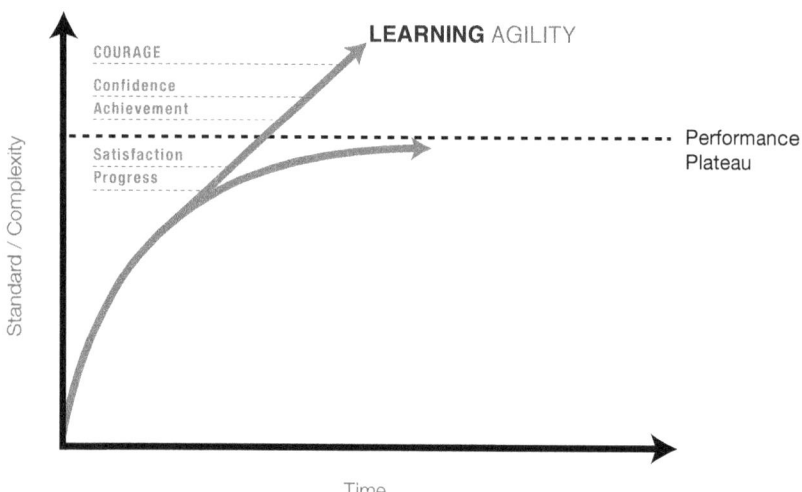

The experience of growth, or the lack of growth, and the feelings that come with it have a powerful influence on our Mindset. When we fail to experience growth, we may come to believe that we can't experience it at all. This belief is what Dweck calls a Fixed Mindset. In fact, in many ways, a Fixed Mindset can be thought of as a Fear Mindset: it makes us fearful of trying new things.

On the other hand, someone who experiences growth, and learns that they can change their abilities, develops what Dweck calls a Growth Mindset. A Growth Mindset can be thought of as a Courage Mindset: it gives us the courage to try new things, and the confidence that we will be able to achieve our goals.

As we will explore in the rest of this book, there are many influences on a person's Mindset. However, the actual experience of growth, or lack of growth, is an extremely powerful one. Understanding these influences – what I call "Mindset Movers" – is a recurring theme throughout *The Agile Learner*. The reason of this is because the Growth Mindset forms the foundation of Learning Agility.

Mindset: The Foundation of the Agile Learner

In our exploration of the Agile Learner, Mindset forms the base of our diagram. This is not because it is the least-important aspect, but because Mindset forms the foundation of Learning Agility.

We begin our exploration of Learning Agility in Section 2 by concentrating on Mindset. We do this because without the understanding that we are capable of growth, we tend not to engage in the actions that would lead us to grow. If we are trapped by a fear of failure, and are unwilling to attempt something difficult, our inaction becomes a self-fulfilling prophecy. Our abilities won't, and don't, change.

> As you will discover, a Growth Mindset is not growth. It is not even necessary for growth to take place. A Growth Mindset is simply the understanding that you are capable of growth. To develop our abilities, we must take the right sort of actions, and our Mindset determines if we are willing to take these actions or not.

In Section 3, we'll explore the Four Rules About Talent that describe the actions we must take to develop our abilities.

The point of developing Learning Agility is so that students can experience more success in their lives. We want students to be able to successfully overcome the challenges they are confronted with in the disruptive world we live in. We want them to have choice in their lives, and to be able to pursue and achieve their goals. And this, of course, raises an interesting question: what do we mean by success?

What Do We Mean by Success?

Success is one of those words people like to argue about. Do you have to be rich to be successful? Do you have to be famous? Do you have to be the best at something?

I often ask people to name someone they consider characteristically successful, and tell me why they consider that person successful.

Try that now. Before reading on, think of someone you consider characteristically successful. Ask yourself why you consider them so successful. Have you done that?

The responses I receive are remarkably similar, no matter who I ask. The people we consider successful tend to have these characteristics:

- They have overcome challenges. They haven't done easy things, they've done hard things.
- The challenges they've overcome have been ones that many people struggle with. We admire people for doing what we haven't or couldn't.
- They have continued to grow throughout their lives. Sometimes they have continued to grow in one domain, which has made

them "the best" at something. Often, they have grown in different aspects of their lives, e.g. their relationship, career(s), contribution to the community, parenting. We admire these people because they are more "rounded".
- They have overcome unique or significant challenges. Perhaps they have started from a place of disadvantage, or they have had a setback (or two), but they haven't been defeated. They have persisted and overcome their setbacks.
- They are not necessarily rich or famous, although they can be. And they're not necessarily the best. Sometimes they aren't even people we like, but we still recognise that what they've done is impressive.

Two things strike me every time I have this conversation. First, there is remarkably little disagreement. We have no trouble identifying the basic characteristics that define success. Secondly, it is almost always *other people* we consider to be characteristically successful.

We recognise and admire characteristically successful people. We buy books about them. We talk about them with our friends and colleagues. But we tend to admire them *from a distance.*

Sure, we have our own successes, yet we rarely consider ourselves successful. Our challenges haven't been as great, or we haven't overcome them as consistently. We feel that we haven't experienced as much growth as the other people we consider *characteristically* successful.

What most people tend to do when they talk about characteristically successful people is put them on the other side of the "Greatness Gap". And this idea of the Greatness Gap, one that is repeated constantly in our society, is a recurring theme in this book, because it is at the heart of the Fixed Mindset.

The Greatness Gap

Professor Dweck (2006, p. 90) expresses the idea of the Greatness Gap like this:

> We like to think of our champions and idols as superheroes who were born different from us. We don't like to think of them as relatively ordinary people who made themselves extraordinary. Why not? To me that is so much more amazing.

When we think of successful people as champions or idols, we attribute their success to *who they are*, rather than *what they've done*. This is what creates the Greatness Gap. We are on one side, and they are on the other. In thinking this way, we excuse ourselves not only of the responsibility, but the mere possibility, of ever achieving what they have done. We tell ourselves, "That's great for them, but *I'm not like them*, so you *can't expect that of me*."

The Greatness Gap is at the heart of the Fixed Mindset. People with a Fixed Mindset believe that what others achieve is a result of who they are, not what they have done.

The Greatness Gap takes away your choice. When you believe that certain goals, achievements and abilities are fundamentally beyond your reach, you lose the choice to pursue them. Doors close to you. You're left searching for where you fit in the world, and working out what you can and can't do, rather than making yourself into the type of person you want to be.

The Growth Mindset understands that there is no Greatness Gap. What one person has achieved, another person can achieve – if they learn to behave in the same way*. For the person with a Growth Mindset, the world is full of choice. Every door is open to them. The person with a Growth Mindset understands they can make themselves into the sort of person they want to become.

The behaviours we see Fixed Mindset people engage in are symptoms of their belief in the Greatness Gap. They don't see that they have the power to choose the course of their life. If we want to make enduring differences to the way students see the world, we must change this underlying belief.

But before we talk about how we change beliefs and build an understanding of how we achieve growth, we need to delve deeper into Mindsets.

As we will discuss, circumstance and opportunity also play a role. This work does not purport to say that anyone can be anything. It demonstrates that there's nothing about who you are that stops you improving. More on this in section 4.

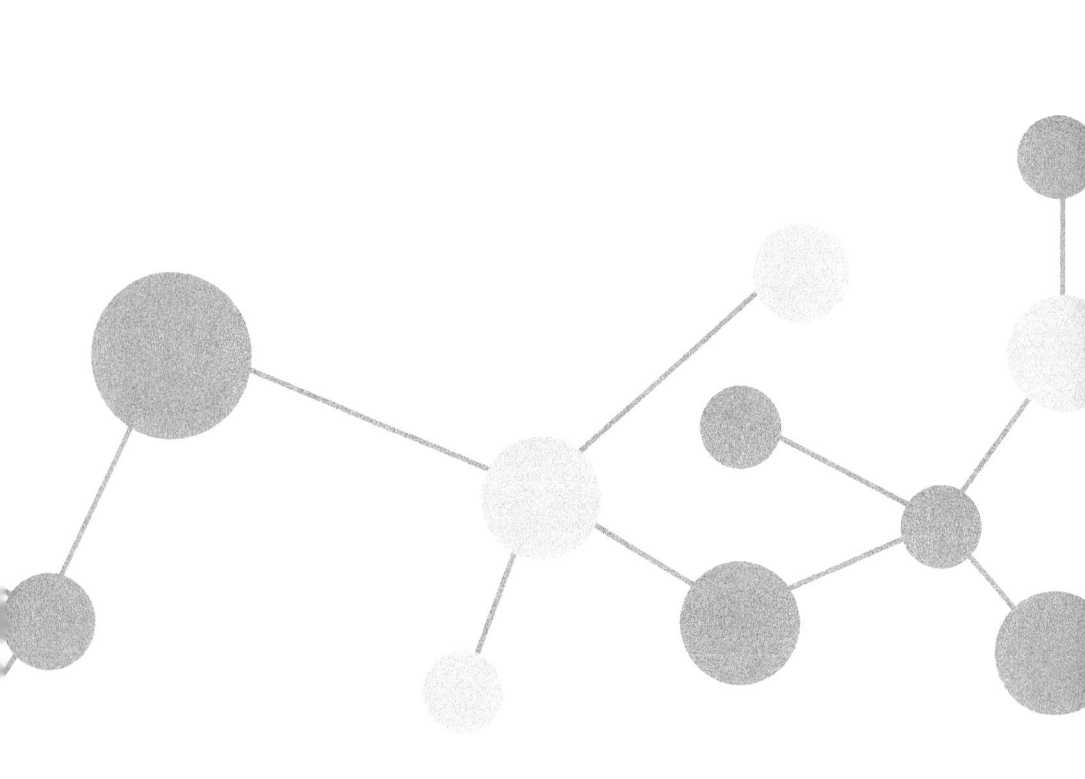

SECTION 2
Mindsets

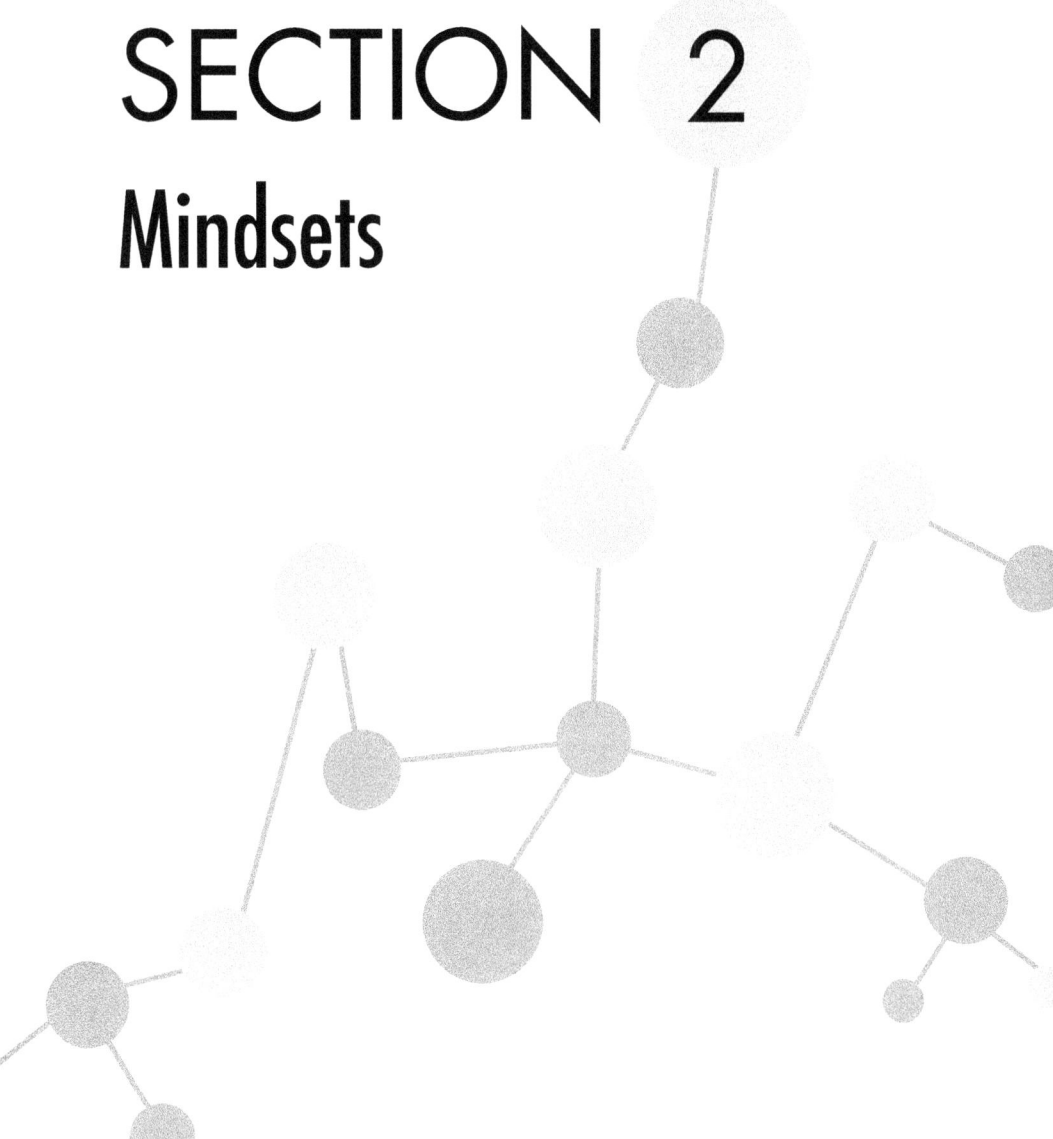

SECTION 2.1
Why Mindset Is Important

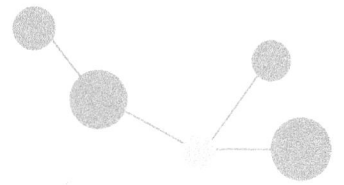

The Fixed and Growth Mindsets

Professor Carol Dweck has spent her career looking at how a person's Mindset – their beliefs about their most basic characteristics, such as intelligence, talents and abilities – affects their motivation, choices and, ultimately, their achievements. She has studied adults as well as children, and describes two basic Mindsets: Fixed and Growth.

The Fixed Mindset – Who Am I?

Students with a Fixed Mindset see their basic characteristics as unchanging. They are smart, or they're not. They have talents, or they don't. They are good at maths, or they aren't. They consider that the abilities they have now will remain much the same for the rest of their lives. Students with a Fixed Mindset "know" which side of the Greatness Gap they were born on.

For students with a Fixed Mindset, life is about discovering themselves. They expect to spend their lives figuring out who they are and where they fit in the world. Finding out who they are determines what they can do in life. So, for someone with a Fixed Mindset, to do "X", you must be an "X" sort of person. If you're not that sort of person, don't bother trying. Go find what you're good at.

Students with a Fixed Mindset consider that personality tests, intelligence tests and aptitude tests identify and define the type of person they are. Measurements of all types categorise them as *being* a certain type of person. This measurement is definitive and final.

To the person with a Fixed Mindset, people fit into different categories. Some people are musicians because they are, and always have been, musical. That's why they can play music. People who create art are artistic people. That's why they can create art. Fixed Mindset students are continually looking for which category they fit into, so they know what type of person they are.

But this search also has the inverse effect – it tells them which categories they don't belong in. Once you know what sort of person you are, you also know what sort of person you're not. Knowing that you don't belong to a particular category means you'd be wasting your time doing the kinds of things people in that category do. If you're not a musical person, there's no point in trying to learn music. Knowing your abilities also defines your inabilities, and limits your choices in life.

> For the Fixed Mindset student, *being* comes before *doing*.

Appearances become critically important. Fixed Mindset students believe that because they can't change themselves, all they can do is change the way others perceive them. For these students, it's more important to look good and say you can do something, rather than try and risk failure.

The Growth Mindset – Who Do I Want to Become?

On the other hand, students with a Growth Mindset see themselves as changeable. They understand that they can change their most basic characteristics. They can learn to become more intelligent, develop talents and create new abilities. For these people, life isn't about discovering who they are and where they fit in the world. For them, life is about discovering what they want to do with their lives and making themselves into the sort of people who can achieve the life they want.

> For the Growth Mindset student, *becoming* comes before *being*.

Students with a Growth Mindset understand that people are different. But, unlike Fixed Mindset students, they don't attribute that difference to people being "born that way". They understand that people have chosen to *make* themselves that way. They've done something to create their abilities and become that sort of person.

For these students, it is not about categorising people as "being" different, but rather recognising the process – the backstory – that led them to specialise and develop abilities in their chosen area. A musician isn't good at playing music because they were born musical. They learnt how to play music, thus becoming musical.

Students with a Growth Mindset aren't worried about being measured by a test. Instead, they use them to help guide their learning. They understand that tests don't tell them anything important about who they are, and that all they tell them is where they might be at that point in time. If they want to be better at something, they know how to use the results of the test to learn how to achieve their goal.

Appearances are less important to people with a Growth Mindset. They aren't focused on looking good; they are focused on making themselves better. If they can't achieve what they want today, that's okay. They'll change so they can do it tomorrow, or the next day. Who they are today is not necessarily who they will be tomorrow.

Choice Versus No Choice

We can point to many differences in the way a student with a Fixed or Growth Mindset sees the world, but at its very heart is choice.

> From the Growth Mindset perspective, people have the choice to change, grow, adapt, learn and become who they want to be. People with a Fixed Mindset don't see that choice. They are locked out of some choices because they see themselves as either being, or not being, that sort of person. They don't see the choice to become.

The consequence of believing in the Greatness Gap is a loss of choice. Once you believe in the Greatness Gap, it takes away your choice to change. For someone with a Growth Mindset, there is a pathway between where they are now, and who they want to be in the future. They may not yet know all the steps, but they know there is a way. When you have a Fixed Mindset, you only see the Greatness Gap. There is no pathway to follow, and no possibility of "becoming".

It is critically important to recognise that students with a Fixed Mindset *don't make bad choices*, although from the outside it may appear that way. They simply don't see a choice in the first place. Understanding this point gives us a fresh new perspective on the difference between the Fixed and Growth Mindset student, which we will explore throughout the rest of this book.

From the Growth Mindset perspective, you choose what you want your life to be. You then make yourself into the sort of person who can achieve that life. The Fixed Mindset perspective doesn't give you this choice.

Understanding the Fixed Mindset Response

From the Fixed Mindset perspective, your basic characteristics can't change much. This basic set of beliefs underlies a set of characteristics that we commonly associate with the Fixed Mindset. But it is the underlying beliefs that define the Fixed Mindset. The outward behaviours are simply the symptoms of these underlying beliefs.

Let's explore some of the common characteristics that result from the belief that you can't change very much:

Challenges are avoided

From the Fixed Mindset perspective, a challenge represents an opportunity to fail. You either have the ability to complete a difficult task, or you don't, and nothing is going to change that. So, your best course of action is to say you can do something and not do anything that might disprove it. Action is your enemy because it has the potential to show others your limitations. Inaction is your friend, because it leaves open the possibility that the challenge is within your abilities.

We often see this in groups that have been labelled. For example, the "gifted" children or the children who have been told they "*are* mathematical". Many teachers have experienced the situation of challenging these students with a difficult task, only to be met with a response of, "I could do that, easily" – with no attempt by the students to actually take on the challenge.

The adage, "It is better to remain silent and be thought a fool than to speak and remove all doubt", may hold true. But for Fixed Mindset students, it is equally true that "it's better to say you can do something and be thought capable than to act and risk being proved wrong".

Giving up is easy

To someone with a Fixed Mindset, giving up appears to be a sensible strategy. Struggle and challenge are a sign of your limitations – that you're not that "type of person" – so any difficulty is a sign that your limits have been reached.

Moreover, because you've reached your "natural" limits, any feeling of struggle is a permanent condition. Something that is hard today, will always be hard.

For the student with a Fixed Mindset, life is about the path of least resistance. Giving up quickly on the tasks they find difficult allows them to focus on the things that come easily.

Effort is a bad thing

The Fixed Mindset views effort as a sign of deficit. Some people do things easily because they were born with their abilities. If you need to put effort into a task, then it's a sign you weren't born with the necessary ability. For the Fixed Mindset student, effort is associated with failure and lack of ability.

This is interesting when viewed in light of the "praise effort" strategies promoted on social media. Being praised for effort, when viewed from the Fixed Mindset perspective, is the same as having your deficits exposed. A teacher's praise that, "You've worked hard today", could be interpreted as, "You've had to work hard today. You don't have the natural ability."

Sometimes, students with a Fixed Mindset will even hide their effort, despite the fact they may be working hard and effectively. They'll either say the task was easy, or attempt to hide the amount of effort they put into their work. These students believe in the adage, "Hard work beats talent, when talent doesn't work very hard". In other words, you only have to work hard when you don't have talent, and you'll never beat a talented person who works hard. This adage reinforces the student's idea that "being" comes before "doing", and that effort is for people who can't do it naturally.

Feedback is ignored

From the Fixed Mindset perspective, it makes sense that you would ignore feedback. Because you believe you can't change much, feedback isn't seen as a way of correcting mistakes, moving forward or setting future learning goals. It simply highlights your deficits. Listening to feedback is like listening to a list of your faults.

One way to identify a student with a Fixed Mindset is to observe their response when they are given back their work. The Fixed Mindset student will want to know what they are good at, and their first reaction will be to focus on what they got right. They tend to ignore the things they got wrong, and any feedback associated with it. For them, mistakes and feedback highlight a deficit that can't be changed, so there's no use dwelling on the negatives.

Students feel threatened by the success of others

From the Fixed Mindset perspective, the world consists of people who can and people who can't. You are either on one side of the Greatness Gap, or you're on the other.

From this perspective, competition and comparisons are potentially negative experiences, and, at the very least, they are permanent. All they do is highlight the type of person you're not, revealing your weaknesses or deficits to the world. The person with a Fixed Mindset usually avoids comparisons, unless they can be used to show their superiority.

Misunderstandings About the Fixed Mindset

We've explored how students with a Fixed Mindset tend to behave: they avoid challenges, they give up easily, they dislike effort, they are threatened by the success of others.

Reading through these behaviours, it's easy to understand why students with a Fixed Mindset are sometimes described as "lazy". It is often assumed that they simply aren't prepared to get off their backsides and do the hard work! But while the characteristics above are accurate, it is inaccurate to label someone with a Fixed Mindset as lazy.

If we are to make a difference to students' Mindsets, we need to go beyond merely describing behaviours. We need to understand that behaviours are *symptoms* – the outward expression of their Mindset. When seen in this light, we realise that there is nothing lazy about someone with a Fixed Mindset.

Let me illustrate the point. I regularly run workshops for teachers about Mindsets. I also previously taught mathematics to middle-years students. Let me compare these two experiences:

Teachers in a Mindset workshop	Children in a mathematics class
I tell participants I have a challenge for them: I want to find out who in the room is tall enough to touch the ceiling.	I tell students I have a challenge for them: a difficult maths problem I want them to solve.
Most people look at me as though I'm stupid for even asking, and stay in their chairs.	Some students look away, find other things to do and don't even start to address the problem.
I repeat the instruction that I want people to stand up and try to touch the ceiling.	I admonish these students, telling them that I expect them to make an effort!

Section 2.1: Why Mindset Is Important

Teachers in a Mindset workshop	Children in a mathematics class
Participants reluctantly stand up. Some wave their hands in the air, resigned to the fact that they can't touch the ceiling.	Some students make half an attempt, not wanting to put too much effort in (at least people might believe they could do it if they tried "properly").
Others make a joke out of the exercise, jumping up and down and laughing at how ridiculous it is.	Others muck around and complain about the task. "It's impossible. No one could do this."
In one workshop, a "vertically challenged" woman outright refused to do the activity (because it would highlight how short she was).	Some students refuse to attempt the problem at all. They tell me it's "too hard" for them.
A few participants try standing on chairs or tables. If they're not tall enough to touch the ceiling, at least they can make it look as though they are taller than they are, and taller than other people in the room.	A few students copy answers from other students. If they can't do the maths, at least they can make others think they can – and do it better than some of the students who truly are trying.

Are the teachers being lazy and unreasonable? Are the students? The answer is that the teachers and the students are behaving perfectly reasonably – given their world view.

From the perspective of someone with a Fixed Mindset, who doesn't believe they can change, it makes perfect sense to not take on the challenge, waste effort trying, or try to look better than their peers even if it involves cheating.

Of course, the height of the adult participants is something that is categorically fixed. All the effort in the world isn't going to make them any taller! So, it is a sensible thing for them to act the way they do. When it comes to fixed traits like height, there really is a Greatness Gap.

The problem is that some of the children, when faced with the maths challenge, behave the same way as the adults. This is because they, incorrectly, believe that their maths ability is similarly fixed.

Understanding the Growth Mindset Response

From the Growth Mindset perspective, the world is vastly different. For these students, the world is about creating themselves. They understand they have the capacity to choose, to become, to change and to develop the abilities that will allow them to be who they want to be. As a result, we see an entirely different set of behaviours.

Challenges are embraced

From a Growth Mindset perspective, you understand that challenging yourself is the only pathway to improvement. Doing easy things that you've already mastered doesn't make you any better. You need to be stretched and challenged by difficult tasks.

While there are times when you need to rehearse and consolidate your learning, you understand that growth comes from trying to do better than your best, making mistakes and learning from them.

Students with a Growth Mindset not only embrace challenges, they often seek them out. Choosing not to be satisfied with the status quo, they look for opportunities to extend and build on their abilities.

Persistence is valued

The Growth Mindset student understands that feelings of struggle and difficulty are temporary. In fact they are good signs, because it's only in struggle and difficulty that they can learn how to behave more intelligently.

It's not that these students enjoy hard work, they just know that it is necessary to experience growth – and they value that growth. They expect to see results at the end of struggle, because they know they can change, and understand things don't stay difficult for ever.

Effort is a good thing

For the student with a Growth Mindset, hard work and effort are what matter most. This is what you must do in order to reach your goals, crossing what someone with a Fixed Mindset would call the Greatness Gap. Effort is associated with growth and success.

While they don't mind getting good grades, they understand that it's what they *did* to earn the grade that's important. *They* weren't being judged, the outcomes of their actions were. Effort is what you've got to put in to become the sort of person that can achieve the grades.

Unlike students with a Fixed Mindset, these students want to be recognised for their effort. They understand that assessment indicates where they are today, but tells them nothing about where they will be tomorrow. Their best guide for future performance is how well they are learning to apply the *right sort of effort* so they can continue to improve.

Seeking, and learning from, feedback

Students with a Growth Mindset expect to make mistakes as they take on difficult challenges. If they didn't make mistakes, then they were probably just learning to do more things, and not achieving better things. To learn from and correct those mistakes, they seek feedback and ask for direction.

Feedback can come in many forms. Sometimes, it's self-directed: students check against a set of established standards or exemplars, self-modifying and self-directing their learning. Other times, they will seek expert guidance. They are continually focused on what they are trying to learn, getting feedback and revisiting their work to fix mistakes and move forward.

The success of others is embraced

From the Growth Mindset perspective, other people's success is an inspiration. It shows what can be achieved and, if they pay attention, how to achieve it. Recognising the great diversity of other people's achievement is proof that anything is possible with the right sort of effort.

For a student with a Growth Mindset, it doesn't matter if the other person's achievement is in an area they are pursuing or not. They understand that what is being rewarded is the effort and the backstory – the "becoming".

Furthermore, the Growth Mindset student doesn't mind competition. Winning or losing, being better or worse than someone else – these things don't say anything permanent about who they are. They simply indicate *where* they are at this point in time. In fact, these students may embrace competition as a way of pushing themselves to new heights.

How Does All This Play Out?

We can see how two students would react to the same situation incredibly differently depending on their Mindset. Imagine a classroom where the teacher sets students a challenging task. Bill is seen to be struggling, so is encouraged by the teacher to continue to work hard. The teacher gives Bill feedback on where he's succeeded, as well as his mistakes and where he should continue to focus his efforts. At the end of the lesson, the teacher uses another student's work as an example of how to solve the problem.

Section 2.1: Why Mindset Is Important

From the Fixed Mindset Perspective

Through the Fixed Mindset lens, this situation may be interpreted quite differently to the way the teacher intended. Bill thinks the teacher is trying to find out who has the ability to solve the problem. Because he struggles, Bill believes he does not have that ability. This is made worse by the fact that he can see that some students were able to solve the problem quickly and with little effort. The teacher highlights this by stating that Bill has to try hard. To make matters worse, the teacher points out exactly which parts Bill can't do. The fact that another student can do the problem, and is singled out for it, highlights Bill's inability.

Next time Bill is confronted with a similar task, his Mindset will tell him to not bother. Bill's previous experience suggests that putting effort into this sort of task will only highlight his deficit. A better approach would be to put in little or no effort, and let people believe he could do it if he worked harder. In that case, he hasn't failed because he "can't" do the work, he has failed because he's "not" doing the work. From his Fixed Mindset perspective, Bill can allow the teacher to believe he could do the work if he tried harder, even though he believes he can't.

From the Growth Mindset Perspective

Mark is looking for a challenge. As he struggles, he is grateful that the teacher recognises he is working hard, reinforcing his conviction that he's working on something difficult enough to learn from. The teacher's feedback helps him focus his efforts, and he begins to make progress, fixing his earlier mistakes. Although he's making headway, by the end of the class Mark hasn't mastered the task yet. Instead of feeling that he doesn't have the ability, he listens carefully to the example of the other student who has mastered the work so that he can learn from it.

The following infographic captures some of the key responses, and the basis for those responses, from the Fixed and Growth Mindset perspectives.

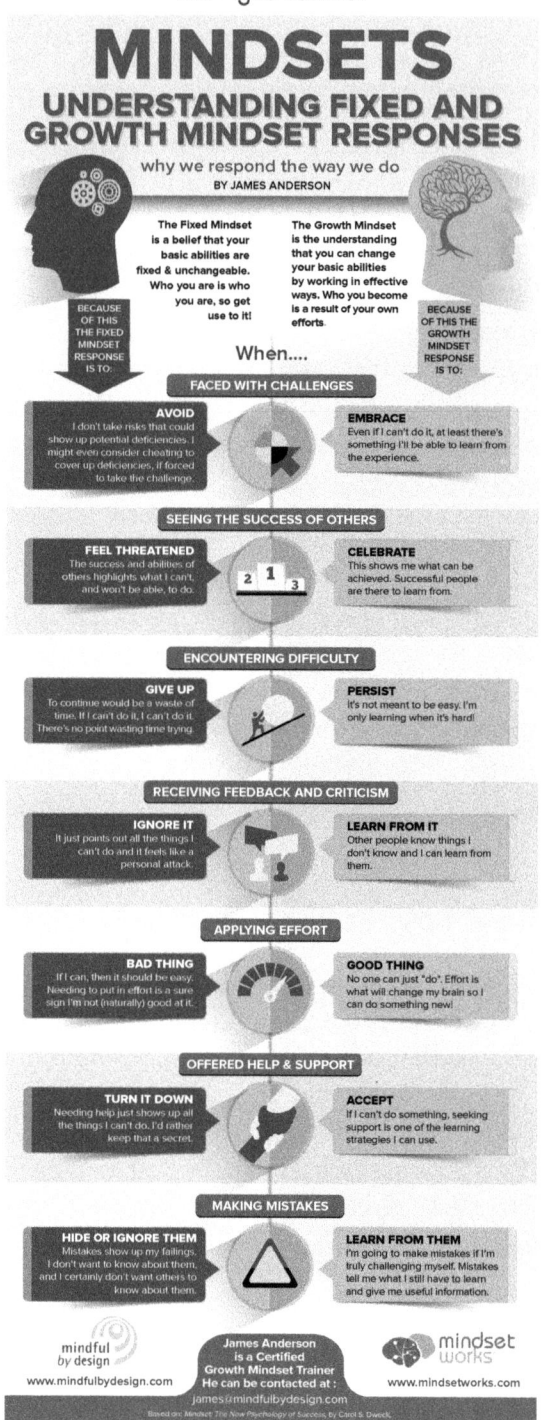

SECTION 2.2
The Mindset Continuum and Mindset Movers

The Mindset Continuum

So much of what you read about Mindsets suggests that there are only two opposing Mindsets: the Fixed Mindset and the Growth Mindset. In fact, up until now, this book has made the same distinction. Contrasting Fixed and Growth is useful to help us understand Mindsets, but to develop practical classroom tools, we need to take a deeper approach.

The reality is that there is a continuum of Mindsets. Fixed and Growth are just two extremes, with many different Mindsets and beliefs in-between. While some people are situated closer to one end of the continuum, most lie somewhere in the middle of those two extremes. Personally, I've never met anyone who I'd describe as having a completely Fixed, or a completely Growth, Mindset!

For example, most students don't either love or hate effort in the way the Fixed/Growth dichotomy would suggest. Most students accept it as necessary. Some see a little bit of effort as good, but sustained effort as bad. Some students enjoy effort, yet others understand it is a pathway to mastery and embrace it. In other words, most students aren't Fixed or Growth: they are somewhere in-between.

The Mindset Continuum, which we will use for the remainder of this book, recognises that people can't be categorised as either Fixed or Growth. This recognition allows us to move to a more meaningful and nuanced understanding of Mindsets, and opens the door to more practical and powerful ways of nurturing students' Mindsets to help them become more Growth Oriented.

The Agile Learner

The Mindset CONTINUUM

Going beyond "Fixed V's Growth" to a deeper understanding of Mindsets

By James Anderson
Certified Growth Mindset Trainer

	FIXED	LOW GROWTH	MIXED	GROWTH	HIGH GROWTH
WORLD VIEW	Sees themselves as **UNCHANGING AND UNCHANGEABLE.** Life is about discovering yourself and searching for where you fit into the world.	Change and **GROWTH IS VERY LIMITED.** See themselves as "not cut out for" some domains. Amount of growth possible in other domains is limited.	Limited Growth Mindset – believes they are capable of **GROWTH IN A LIMITED NUMBER OF DOMAINS.** Life offers only limited choices.	Sees themselves as **CAPABLE OF SIGNIFICANT GROWTH** in most domains. Sees great choice in life. May see themselves as restricted from significant growth in some domains.	Understands they can **CHANGE THEIR MOST BASIC CHARACTERISTICS.** Life is about deciding what you want to be and creating the abilities required to reach goals.
CHALLENGES	**AVOIDS CHALLENGES.** Sees them as a potential threat.	Takes on **EASY CHALLENGES** that they believe they are likely to succeed at.	**PREFERS CLEAR, IMMEDIATE GOALS** that aren't too far out of reach, or in an area they find difficult.	**ENJOYS BEING CHALLENGED** by more open-ended tasks, even if not always immediately successful.	**EMBRACES CHALLENGES** even when path to achievement is not immediately clear.
ENCOUNTERING DIFFICULTY & OBSTACLES	**GIVES UP IMMEDIATELY** when they encounter difficulty.	**TRIES FOR A WHILE,** but gives up if not progressing easily. May try a few alternatives when encountering obstacles.	**PERSISTS WHEN SEEING PROGRESS.** Is developing a repertoire of strategies for getting past obstacles.	**EXPECTS EVENTUAL MASTERY.** Understands new learning is meant to be difficult so sticks at tasks for long periods.	**PERSISTS FOR LONG PERIODS** even in the face of setbacks and when new skills need to be learnt to achieve mastery.
EFFORT	**EFFORT IS ASSOCIATED WITH FAILURE** and inability, so is seen as bad. Expects things you can do to come easily.	Recognizes that effort is sometimes required. **SUSTAINED EFFORT IS A BAD THING.** Misunderstands that not all types of effort produce growth.	**EFFORT IS NECESSARY,** but usually not enjoyable. Likely to prefer to do it easily. Recognizes when effort is being ineffective.	**EFFORT IS A GOOD THING.** Has experienced success as a result of effort in the past. Associates Effective Effort with growth.	Understands **EFFORT AS PATH TO MASTERY.** Actively works on developing strategies for more Effective Effort.
FEEDBACK & CRITICISM	**IGNORES** useful negative feedback. Sees feedback as a list of their faults.	Accepts some direct feedback when corrections can be made quickly and easily. **TENDS TO FOCUS ON POSITIVE FEEDBACK.**	**FORMATIVE FEEDBACK IS SEEN AS USEFUL,** as long as it is targeted and achievable.	Accepts and **LEARNS FROM FEEDBACK.** Positive feedback is seen as recognition of the effort and process that led to the achievement.	**REQUESTS CRITICAL FEEDBACK** from targeted expert sources in order to improve both process and outcome.
SUCCESS OF OTHERS	**FEELS THREATENED** by comparisons to others and avoids competitions, as these may highlight perceived deficits.	**MAY MIS-ATTRIBUTE SUCCESS** of others to luck or natural ability rather than growth achieved through effort.	**ENJOYS PERSONAL SUCCESS,** so will engage in competition and comparison when these make them look good.	**FINDS LESSONS AND INSPIRATION** in the success of others. Admires excellence. Enjoys the challenge posed by competition.	**SEEKS OUT MASTERS AND EXPERTS** in an effort to "learn their secrets". Competition is seen as a way for both competitors to push themselves to improve.
MAKING MISTAKES	Actively **HIDES OR IGNORES** mistakes.	**MAKES EXCUSES** for mistakes. Looks for quick fixes. May attribute blame to others.	Expects to make mistakes and understands **MISTAKES CAN BE CORRECTED.**	Recognizes mistakes made are **SIGNPOSTS FOR LEARNING** opportunities.	Deliberately stretches themselves so errors have **HIGH LEARNING POTENTIAL** to facilitate further growth.
OFFERED HELP AND SUPPORT	**TURNS DOWN** help and support. Feels requiring help highlights their own deficits.	**TOLERATES** help when given. Disinclined to ask for help. Doesn't like to be seen to need help.	**ACCEPTS HELP** and support when offered. May not continue to seek help, if difficulties are persistent.	Expects feedback and recognizes it as **DESIRABLE** to help them grow.	**SEEKS OUT** help and support from specialized sources.

Download this infographic in full size from **www.jamesanderson.com.au/p/TheAgileLearnerDownloads/**

Section 2.2: The Mindset Continuum and Mindset Movers

The characteristics of people at different places along the Mindset Continuum are all reflections of their underlying beliefs. Most students don't see themselves as completely unchanging, or infinitely changeable. Experience tells us that most students have what we might term a "Limited-Growth" Mindset. They understand that they can and do grow, but believe they are limited in either the amount they can grow or by the domains in which they can grow.

Why a Continuum?

The Fixed/Growth Mindset dichotomy was useful to help us understand the "big picture" of Mindsets. But when it comes to discussions about understanding where Mindsets come from, how they affect our decisions on a day-to-day basis and what we need to do to change them, a Mindset Continuum offers us a more powerful tool, and one that more closely matches reality.

Social media often promotes what I call "Mindset Moments". The idea is that you can simply choose to adopt a Growth Mindset when you approach a task, and to a certain degree this is possible and even desirable. We can choose our actions, and when we can choose them through a Growth Mindset lens this is a positive thing to do.

While a Mindset Moment can determine our actions in a moment, they don't usually determine our *reactions*.

> Most of the time, our Mindset is part of what we call our unconscious bias. It guides our actions when we are not paying attention.

And while we can choose to adopt a Mindset Moment action, our reactions reflect our underlying Mindset, which falls somewhere along the Mindset Continuum.

For example, consider the student who seeks out a teacher's feedback to help them with a task. Initially they listen to the feedback as the teacher praises the things they've done well and points out minor errors. Then, as the teacher discovers some major errors in the student's work and begins explaining how to fix them, the student becomes less attentive and, eventually, dismissive. They tell the teacher in a frustrated voice that they can "work it out for themselves" and leave.

What this student is experiencing is a symptom of a Mindset that might be on the Low Growth end of the continuum. They were happy to listen to some feedback, especially when it was positive or pointed out only minor errors. In this circumstance, they could be confident they "were good at" the task. But when the feedback started to point out more serious errors, they first didn't want to hear it, then felt their faults were being pointed out and so avoided further scrutiny, turning down feedback that might have actually helped them.

If the only way we had to describe this student was as having either a Fixed or Growth Mindset, we would be wrong on both counts. Their responses fit neither the Fixed nor Growth Mindset. This student wasn't demonstrating a Fixed or Growth Mindset, but was demonstrating what we might describe as a Low-Growth Mindset. The ability to recognise where a student lies on the continuum allows us to tailor pedagogy to suit their needs.

Changing Mindsets

Slow Shifts or Quick Flips

When we ask students to adopt a Growth Mindset, it's like offering them an aspirin: it treats the symptoms, but not the cause. Students may act as though they have a Growth Mindset, flipping from Fixed to Growth on the teacher's instruction, but the underlying beliefs that guide them when they aren't paying attention are unlikely to have changed.

Section 2.2: The Mindset Continuum and Mindset Movers

If their beliefs haven't changed, then their Mindset hasn't changed. Students are only acting like they have a Growth Mindset because we've told them to. This might feel satisfying for the teacher in a lesson, but is it achieving our long-term goal of developing students who'll carry a Growth Mindset into their adult lives? If we focus on creating Mindset Moments, what happens when we're not there to tell students how to act?

As teachers, we need to think long term. We must ask ourselves: how likely is it that our students will demonstrate the behaviours of a Growth Mindset when we're not there? How likely are they to behave that way next week, next month or next year?

As Professor Carol Dweck (2016) points out, a Growth Mindset is not a declaration, it's a journey. As teachers, we can't "install" a Growth Mindset into students, just as we can't expect them to suddenly adopt a Growth Mindset in all aspects of their lives. Even if students want to have a Growth Mindset, we have to appreciate that whatever Mindset we are currently observing is based on beliefs and assumptions that have been built up over a long period of time, and it's going to take time to challenge, shift and change these ingrained beliefs.

As teachers, we have to nurture students toward an increasingly Growth-Oriented Mindset. This can only take place gradually, and as they change, they will move along the Mindset Continuum.

> Our role as teachers is to develop robust and enduring Growth-Oriented Mindsets in our students.

The Mindset Continuum also helps us to understand the nature of this work in schools. If teachers assume that all students fall into one of two Mindsets, either Fixed or Growth, and their job is to ensure students have a Growth Mindset, then we set ourselves up for failure. It is unreasonable to expect teachers to have students suddenly displaying a Growth Mindset. A more realistic expectation is for teachers to create experiences that over time help slowly shift a student's Mindset towards an increasingly Growth-Oriented one.

> Our success as Growth Mindset teachers is not measured by the number of students in our class with a Growth Mindset. Rather, it is measured by how much more Growth Oriented we have helped our students to become.

As students become more Growth Oriented, they persist for longer, take on more and greater challenges, are receptive to more feedback and, bit by bit, begin to close the Greatness Gap.

Changing students' Mindsets, little by little along the Mindset Continuum, is a journey that teachers will nurture for many, many years.

If a Mindset is not like a light switch, unable to be flipped between Fixed and Growth in Mindset Moments, then how do we go about nudging students along the Mindset Continuum? To answer that, we must ask another question: where does our Mindset come from in the first place, and how do we go about changing the one we have?

Mindset Movers

We aren't born with a Mindset. Rather, it is built up over time from a wide range of influences called "Mindset Movers". A Mindset Mover can be either positive, pushing us towards a more Growth-Oriented Mindset, or it can be negative, pushing us towards the fixed end of the Mindset Continuum.

Section 2.2: The Mindset Continuum and Mindset Movers

Students experience Mindset Movers every day: at home, at school and through their lived experience. Mindset Movers are experiences that tell us something about how much change we are capable of. In other words, they help establish our Mindset.

Although these Mindset Movers occur all the time, they often go unnoticed. They might be as overt as a student being told they are "smart", or they may be as subtle as a tone of voice. They may be embedded in structures in the school, or reflected in the storyline of a book. They may come from parents, teachers or other students, but no matter where they come from, they very often pass unnoticed, and unchallenged. They can be subtle, and are not as overt as Mindset Moments, but each one adds up.

For example, the adage, "Hard work beats talent, when talent doesn't work very hard", is an example of a negative Mindset Mover. If it goes unchallenged, the message – that some people have talent, and the rest of us have to work hard to make up for our lack of natural talent – implies that a Greatness Gap exists. If we accept this message, our Mindset experiences a little nudge toward the fixed end of the continuum. I worked with a principal who had used this phrase his entire career in an effort to encourage students to work hard, without realising that he was unintentionally telling them that natural talent existed, and that their efforts proved they didn't have any.

On the other hand, if a student tries something very difficult and succeeds, they experience growth. This experience acts as a positive Mindset Mover. The student comes to understand that they are capable of (some) change, and they experience a little nudge toward the growth end of the Mindset Continuum.

Adopting a Growth Mindset in a Mindset Moment can lead students to experience some of the benefits of the Growth Mindset, and these benefits may act as positive Mindset Movers, which, of course, is a good thing. So, strategies that ask students to adopt a Growth Mindset do have their place in a teacher's Growth Mindset repertoire. But they are not everything.

> Our job as teachers is to create experiences that slowly shift a student toward an increasingly Growth-Oriented Mindset.

As educators, our job is to implement regular, consistent, positive Mindset Movers to slowly shift, not flip, a student's Mindset. Each small, positive Mindset Mover we employ nudges a student towards an increasingly Higher-Growth Orientation. At the same time, we also need to be aware of the negative Mindset Movers that surround students, and seek to reduce them.

By building many positive Mindset Movers into our day-to-day practice, and removing the negative ones, we slowly change students' underlying beliefs and understandings. Our goal is not for students to adopt a Growth Mindset for one lesson, but rather to build robust, Growth-Oriented Mindsets that endure. This can only be achieved by addressing students' underlying beliefs – treating the cause, not the symptoms.

> Where we find ourselves on the Mindset Continuum is the sum total of all the positive and negative Mindset Movers we have experienced in our lives. This is not to suggest that all Mindset Movers are equal, they aren't, but it does mean that they all matter.

As we delve deeper into what working with Mindsets looks like in schools and the classroom, we will call again and again on the Mindset Continuum and the concept of Mindset Movers. We'll look at how our words and actions in the classroom, and at home, act as Mindset Movers, shifting students along the Mindset Continuum.

We will continue to explore positive and negative Mindset Movers throughout this book. They are, after all, what our pedagogy will be built on. But for now, it is worth noting the major categories that Mindset Movers fall into. Being familiar with these will help us become better at identifying them in our classrooms and in the community.

Mindset Movers – The Essential Five

While there are many examples of Mindset Movers, both positive and negative, we can broadly categorise them into five key messages. Below I briefly outline each one, highlight some key points and some social memes that exemplify several of them. There is great complexity and subtlety in each that we'll continue to explore.

1. **Growth**
    - Negative Mindset Mover: The amount of growth you're capable of achieving is limited, e.g. "Not everyone can be good at that". Some people have less "potential" than others.
    - Positive Mindset Mover: There is no limit to what you can achieve. Your potential is unlimited. Learning is a way of growing your brain!

2. **Effort**
    - Negative Mindset Mover: It takes less effort for some people to improve than others. Some people just find it easier. "Hard work will beat talent, (but only) when talent doesn't work very hard."

- Positive Mindset Mover: Effort is not simply equal to time and energy. If you're putting in effort, and not experiencing growth, then it's the wrong sort of effort! Change the way you're working and you can experience as much growth as anyone.

3. **Practice**
    - Negative Mindset Mover: Some people don't have to practice as much, e.g. the overnight success. Or the limiting phrase that "it's okay, as long as you tried your hardest."
    - Positive: "The 'overnight' part of the overnight success is just the sudden recognition of years of hard work." Perfect practice makes perfect. Practice isn't a matter of turning up, it's how you practice that makes all the difference. Practicing in the right way makes things possible that were impossible before!

4. **Innate Differences**
    - Negative Mindset Mover: People are born different. Some people aren't cut out for that.
    - Positive Mindset Mover: You have the power to become the sort of person you want to be.

5. **Naturals**
    - Negative Mindset Mover: There are people who are born with natural abilities and special gifts. They can't control whether or not they have them, they just do. Discover your own natural abilities.
    - Positive Mindset Mover: We are what we make ourselves to be.

SECTION 2.3
Teacher Mindset

The Power of Teacher Mindset

Teachers have a powerful opportunity to influence students' Mindsets by creating Mindset Movers through almost every aspect of their pedagogy, but it is not simply a matter of the words we use. Mindset Movers can be created through what's valued in the classroom, how and when praise is given, how assessment is carried out, how the classroom is arranged, and which school structures are in place – such as recognition and reward systems. The actions teachers take, or don't take, all have the potential to create positive or negative Mindset Movers.

The burgeoning awareness of the importance of Growth Mindsets means more teachers are making a deliberate effort to increase the number of positive Mindset Movers in the classroom. They are adopting the Growth Mindset as a pedagogical tool, utilising strategies such as process and effort praise. Terms such as "not yet" are being used, and there is an increasing focus on growth and the process of learning. These are just some of the many strategies being employed that are teaching students about the importance of the Growth Mindset.

All the above, and many more, are good pedagogical tools that can create positive Mindset Movers. The difficulty comes when teachers "adopt" a Growth Mindset without first reflecting deeply on their own Mindset.

Recall that our Mindset is part of our unconscious bias. It filters our perceptions and drives our actions when we are not paying attention. While teachers can choose to adopt a strategy, closer examination might reveal an inconsistency between intentional Growth Mindset pedagogy and other actions taken during the day.

For example, imagine a teacher who has adopted the Growth Mindset and deliberately praises effort in the classroom in order to create a positive Mindset Mover. But if this teacher unconsciously holds more fixed views about abilities – for example, they see some students as having more potential than others – this strategy might unintentionally be translated into "praise the *struggling* students for their effort".

In this context, the Mindset Mover created is that only weak students need to put in effort while other students get the work done easily. Praising effort becomes the consolation prize, and effort becomes a bad thing – something that illustrates you can't achieve things easily. This would be an extremely negative Mindset Mover, and an unintended consequence of the teacher's Low-Growth Mindset.

The False Mindset

This type of inconsistency is what Professor Dweck and her colleague Susan Mackie (2016) call the "False Mindset". Someone with a False Mindset advocates the Growth Mindset, but their actions reflect a more fixed view of abilities.

The False Mindset poses a significant challenge in schools and classrooms, and emphasises just how important it is that we have a thorough understanding of Mindsets. Teachers can't simply "adopt" a set of Growth Mindset behaviours without reflecting deeply on their own beliefs.

John Hattie on Mindsets – 0.19

At the 2015 Annual Visible Learning Conference in San Antonio, Texas, Professor John Hattie discussed the effect size – a way of ranking various influences on learning and achievement – of Fixed versus Growth Mindset. He found that the effect size of the Fixed versus Growth

Mindset on student performance was 0.19, well below his critical hinge point of 0.40. Taken at face value, an effect size of 0.19 suggests that our work with Mindsets does not have a significant impact on student performance.

But Hattie also pointed out that the reason for this effect size was because most adults have a Fixed Mindset, and treat students accordingly. He wasn't suggesting that we shouldn't be working towards developing Growth Mindsets in students. In fact, he was advocating that, to do it well, our work with Mindsets must go deeper by cultivating a more meaningful understanding of how talents and abilities are developed.

> In many respects, Hattie was saying that to have an impact on students' Mindsets, we must first work on teachers' Mindsets.

Hattie didn't use the term False Mindset, but it is exactly what he was talking about.

False Mindset: Causes and Cure

You only need to look at the way social media portrays Mindsets to see how Fixed and Growth Mindsets have become polarised and stigmatised. This stigmatisation of the Fixed Mindset is an underlying cause of the False Mindset.

Fixed is red, and Growth is green. Positive images are associated with the Growth Mindset, while negative images are associated with the Fixed Mindset. We are left with a combative way of thinking, in which Growth Mindsets win and Fixed Mindsets lose.

When Dweck's work burst onto the educational scene a few years ago, the Growth Mindset was clearly what teachers were "meant to have". Teachers were given a (false) choice: do you have a Growth Mindset or a Fixed Mindset? Most teachers adopted a (good) Growth Mindset and, with that declaration, there was no need for further examination.

The reality is that few teachers (or anyone else) have a Growth Mindset. And by the same token, not many teachers have a Fixed Mindset, either. The majority are somewhere in between, but "in between" doesn't exist in the Fixed versus Growth dichotomy we're usually presented with.

The truth is that the Mindset you have is neither good nor bad. It's not something you have chosen. It just is. Your Mindset is the sum of all the Mindset messages you've received throughout your life.

> What is important is that you're able to recognise where your Mindset lies along the Mindset Continuum, and work towards making it even more Growth Oriented.

The Mindset Continuum is a powerful tool because it allows us to recognise that simply because we don't have a Growth Mindset, doesn't necessarily mean we have a Fixed Mindset either. In fact, everyone has a Growth Mindset, but some people are more highly Growth Oriented than others. Wherever you find yourself along the Mindset Continuum today is not "wrong", it is the foundation upon which you can build an even stronger Growth-Oriented Mindset.

The Mindset Continuum allows teachers to be more honest and accurate in the evaluation of their own Mindset. Recognising the Mindset Movers they have experienced throughout life helps teachers examine the causes of their underlying beliefs, and allows them to question some of those beliefs – the cause of their Mindset – and challenge them.

Until teachers – and all adults – look critically at their underlying beliefs, we will continue to send mixed and conflicting messages to our children. While we can intentionally adopt Growth Mindset strategies, our deeper beliefs are being communicated through our unconscious bias.

The Power of the False Mindset and Negative Mindset Movers

Let me give you a true example of the power of the False Mindset, and the impact of negative Mindset Movers:

At school, James always admired the music and drama students. They were the cool kids. Their performances on stage were amazing. But as much as he loved what they did, James never once went to an audition. He never learnt an instrument, because he knew he wasn't a musical person.

Early in his first year of secondary school, James was in music class and the students were learning to play the drums. He thought it was a lot of fun, with different groups of students playing different rhythms. The room was full of ta-ta-ti-ti and he was engaged and enjoying the work.

At the end of the lesson, the teacher told the class he had a challenge for them. He wanted them to try to play one rhythm on their left hand, and a different rhythm on their right hand. Excitedly, the students tried the task – and all of them failed. Everyone had a laugh and went to the next class.

James went home, inspired by the class, and was determined to work out how to play the two rhythms simultaneously. He developed his own strategy to help him learn. He rolled out a large piece of paper on the kitchen bench, and wrote the rhythm for his right hand on the top of the page. He then wrote the rhythm for his left hand underneath. This allowed him to see the pattern of the two rhythms together. By walking along the bench, he could work out when he should use his left hand, right hand or both hands.

The next day, having mastered this pattern, he showed the music teacher. "Was this the rhythm you wanted us to do in class?" James proceeded to perform the two rhythms perfectly – the teacher's face lit up. "Wow! That's amazing. How did you do that?" he asked. James told the teacher how he had worked out a strategy, and spent hours practicing.

The teacher's face softened as he said, "Oh. So, you can't *really* do it, then. But it's great to see you working hard."

The teacher was trying to be encouraging – "*It's great to see you working hard.*" – but it was a consolation prize. The underlying message was that James *had to* work hard to find a strategy to make up for the fact that he couldn't really do the task – at least, not in the way a "musical person" would have done it.

From that point on, James "knew" he wasn't musical, because he just wasn't that type of person. He'd been categorised. Apparently, there were people in the world who could tap out two different rhythms easily, and there were other people who could also do it, but they had to work harder. James now knew which sort of person he was, so he never went to an audition or took up an instrument. That door was closed to him. Instead, he listened to the teachers who said he was more naturally mathematical and scientific, and searched those fields for where he fitted in the world.

(Any similarity between this character and the author is *not* coincidental.)

Section 2.3: Teacher Mindset

Belief, Reality and Action

Carol Dweck (2006) defines the Growth Mindset as the *belief* that your most basic characteristics are malleable. In short, it is a belief in your own ability to change. Professor Dweck and others have repeatedly demonstrated that having a Growth Mindset can significantly increase student performance, motivation and resilience.

For me, the most interesting aspect of this work is not that a Growth Mindset makes a difference, but why and how this *belief* should make a difference. Why does a *belief* matter? And what's the mechanism through which the Growth Mindset works? How is the actual *growth* achieved?

Recall that I asked my workshop participants to stand and try to touch the ceiling. They couldn't do it. If they had believed more in their ability to grow taller, would their efforts have created the growth they desired? Would they have grown? No! I believe in gravity. Experience tells me that if I jump off the roof of my house, I'll fall to the ground and injure myself. But if I decided to stop believing in gravity, would it stop me from falling? No!

Although these examples seem trivial, they have a critical point: *beliefs don't work*. It's not the belief that matters, it's the underlying reality.

Believing in something that is not true does not change reality. It doesn't matter how much you believe you'll grow taller if you try hard enough. It doesn't change the fact that, as adults, we can't change our height. Likewise, refusing to believe that something is real does not stop it being real. If I refused to accept that gravity exists, I'm still going to fall to the ground if I jump off the roof of my house.

> The reason a Growth Mindset works is not because of the belief, but rather the underlying reality that we *are* capable of growth.

If we were not capable of growth, if our abilities – or the limits to our abilities – were fixed at birth, then believing otherwise would not change that underlying reality, and Dweck and other researchers would not have been able to show such significant improvements in student outcomes.

Belief Matters – But It Isn't Everything

The belief in your ability to grow is important, but it's not enough.

It is essential to recognise that a Growth Mindset is only *associated* with growth: it is *not required* for growth, and it *does not guarantee* it. A Growth Mindset does not "cause" growth.

There are plenty of people with a Fixed Mindset who experience significant growth and success. If a Growth Mindset was essential for growth, we would not see people such as retired tennis ace John McEnroe, or some high-achieving children who have been labelled as "gifted and talented", displaying characteristically Fixed Mindsets.

Likewise, there are plenty of people with a Growth Mindset who do not experience the growth they would like. The self-help industry is a testament to this fact. People wouldn't buy self-help books if they didn't want to change, and didn't believe that change was possible. Yet many people invest in books and courses only to see little, if any, results.

A Growth Mindset tells us, "I can grow." It doesn't tell us how to achieve growth.

Section 2.3: Teacher Mindset

> We must learn not only that we are capable of growth, but also how to achieve that growth.

Action is Key

A Growth Mindset works because of the underlying reality that we are capable of change. But the mechanism through which a Growth Mindset leads to growth is *action*.

A Growth Mindset makes a difference because it *invites us to act*. It tells us that we are capable of change, and encourages us to make the choice to grow.

Recall that at the heart of the Growth Mindset is choice. Unlike the person with a Fixed Mindset, who believes they must find where they fit in the world, the person with a Growth Mindset can choose to become the sort of person they want to be. And with this comes the choice *not to change*.

Having the ability to change does not mean it is imperative to change. From the Growth Mindset perspective, you can choose not to take action. Therefore, you don't grow in the areas you don't want to pursue. Understanding that you are capable of growth does not cause growth – it gives you the choice to grow.

For example, today, although I understand that I could develop my abilities in music I choose not to. Instead, I focus my time and limited resources in other areas. That's a choice I can make, freely, with a Growth Mindset.

Unfortunately, simply taking action does not necessarily result in growth, either. Someone with a Growth Mindset who engages in the wrong sort of actions will not grow.

Furthermore, someone with a Fixed Mindset is capable of just as much growth as someone with a Growth Mindset. They might see themselves as fixed, and so be less likely to engage in action that could lead to growth, but if they are encouraged to take the right sort of action, they will still experience growth.

In this light, it is clear that the teacher's responsibility is to teach students that they are capable of growth, as well as *how* to achieve it. As I have said, simply believing in growth is not enough. Teachers must ensure that their students gain an understanding of the types of action that will lead to growth.

> Just believing you can grow isn't enough. You also have to be taught how to grow, and that's the job of the teacher.

Beliefs and Understandings

When we assume, incorrectly, that the mechanism through which a Growth Mindset works is belief, our pedagogy becomes focused solely on building students' belief. Our classrooms become filled with positive affirmations, slogans and catch phrases, and growth is not achieved.

But when we focus on teaching students an understanding of, and the capacity to engage in, the actions that lead to growth, we see two important outcomes. First, by engaging in the right sort of actions, students experience growth in their abilities. This growth acts as a powerful positive Mindset Mover, helping them develop an increasingly Growth-Oriented Mindset. Secondly, by increasing our understanding of how we achieve growth, we help dispel the myths and misunderstandings about how talents and abilities develop. We remove the influence of negative Mindset Movers.

Our work with Growth Mindsets must not focus on *beliefs*. Rather, we need to focus on *understanding*. We need to understand the underlying reality that growth is possible, and how it is achieved.

Carol Dweck understood this when she first tried to develop a more Growth-Oriented Mindset in students. Her approach wasn't to create posters that said, "Have these Growth Mindset characteristics", like much of social media would lead us to believe is the best approach. Her approach was to teach students "Brainology", which is one of the underlying realities that underscore why we are capable of growth.

The Agile Learner not only understands that growth is possible, they also know how to achieve it. So, to develop Agile Learners, we need to delve into how growth is achieved using the Four Rules About Talent.

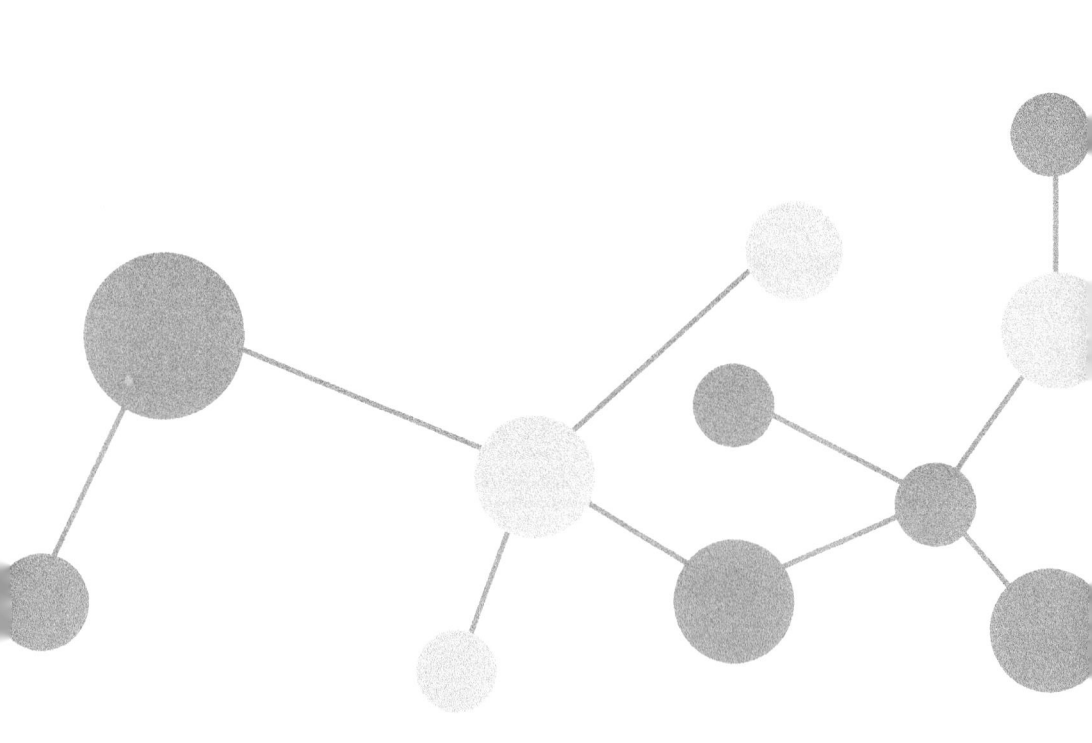

SECTION 3
How Do We Achieve Growth?

SECTION 3
How Do We Achieve Growth?

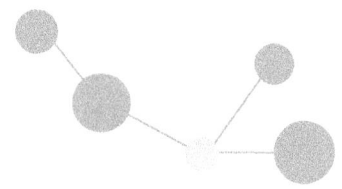

The Four Rules About Talent

If we are capable of significant growth – if our abilities, talents and even intelligence are not fixed qualities – the essential question must be: how do we achieve growth?

To answer this, we will draw on research into the process through which excellence is developed, as well as the behaviours required to engage in this process effectively. Our exploration will encompass modern understandings of intelligence, and unpack the implications of research into the amazing plasticity of our brain.

From this research, we derive the Four Rules About Talent:
1. You have CHOICE.
2. You must PRACTICE.
3. It takes EFFORT.
4. Growth is UNLIMITED.

Understanding these rules is the pathway to developing our talents and abilities, and, ultimately, achieving more with our lives.

Of course, as we've discussed, our Mindset plays a foundational role in the development of our abilities. So, as we explore each of the Four Rules, we will consider how the messages we communicate about them can act as Mindset Movers. When we understand and accurately convey the rules, we create positive Mindset Movers that contribute to the Growth Mindset. On the other hand, if we misunderstand and miscommunicate these rules, we generate negative Mindset Movers that contribute to the Fixed Mindset.

The Study of Exceptional Performance

The past 30 years have seen unprecedented advances in our understanding of how talents and abilities are developed. These ideas have been explored and popularised in books such as Malcolm Gladwell's *Outliers* (Little, Brown and Company, 2008), Geoff Colvin's *Talent is Overrated* (Portfolio, 2008) and Daniel Coyle's *The Talent Code* (Bantam Books, 2009), to name a few. But behind these popular accounts lies the pervading influence of Professor Anders Ericsson's research.

Professor Ericsson has spent his career leading the field of Acquisition of Excellence, studying the process through which peak performers in fields as diverse as memory, medicine, music and chess have achieved their talents and abilities. What he has discovered is that the development of these abilities, far from being the result of innate gifts, is the result of a special form of practice that he calls "Deliberate Practice". Deliberate Practice involves stepping outside of your Comfort Zone and attempting to do better than your best. It involves focusing on specific performance tasks, getting feedback on your progress from an expert or a clear set of standards and acting to fix mistakes. We'll explore this in more detail later.

Ericsson's work is powerful, so much so that several authors have interpreted it to mean that all you need to do to achieve excellence is engage in Deliberate Practice. But as exciting as Ericsson's work is, simply describing the process that peak performers engage in is not the same as saying that anyone can follow the same process and achieve equally high results.

The skyrocketing number of self-help books on shelves today illustrates that there are plenty of people who want to achieve higher performance. But many – perhaps most – end up reaching a Performance Plateau, where they find further growth difficult. In other words, there is more to continuous growth and achieving excellence than Deliberate Practice.

Section 3: How Do We Achieve Growth?

The work of Art Costa and Bena Kallick gives us a critical insight into how peak performance is achieved. Costa and Kallick's research differs from Ericsson's in one key aspect: instead of looking at the *process* that leads to excellence, they investigate the *behaviours* peak performers demonstrate when engaging in that process.

Costa and Kallick describe these behaviours as Habits of Mind. Their work is based on the meta-analysis of the behaviours of people who perform at the peak of their fields. They define Habits of Mind as the dispositions that are skilfully and mindfully employed by characteristically successful people when confronted with problems, the solutions to which are not immediately apparent. Put slightly differently, the Habits of Mind describe the behaviours of top performers as they engage in the difficult tasks necessary for the process of growth.

While leaders such as Ericsson, Costa and Kallick have been unpacking the mysteries of peak performance, great strides have been made in other areas of our understanding of human performance.

Intelligence is undoubtedly associated with peak performance, because peak performers behave intelligently. Indeed, for most of the past century, "being" intelligent was considered a prerequisite for success in many areas. In the 40s and 50s, researchers such as Lewis Terman tried to demonstrate that an individual's innate intelligence could predict future performance, but this line of research broadly failed. More recent research by leaders, such as developmental psychologist Howard Gardner, has transformed our understanding of intelligence from being a static, general and largely inherited trait, to a dynamic and diverse characteristic that we are all capable of developing.

Finally, breakthroughs in our understanding of the functioning of the brain have given the above research a neurological basis. While the work of the great minds listed above describes what is possible in terms of the capacity for human achievement, our growing understanding of the brain's ability to rewire itself gives us a deeper understanding of the underlying cause of enhanced performance.

Taken together, these diverse fields weave a powerful and coherent picture of what it takes to develop Learning Agility and, ultimately, our talents and abilities. In the coming sections, we will consider how this research yields the Four Rules About Talent, exploring the way they are applied in schools and classrooms and how an understanding of them contributes to the development of our Mindset.

SECTION 3.1
The Rule of Choice

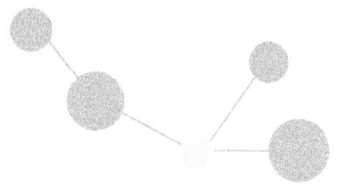

As we have previously explored, choice is at the heart of the Growth Mindset. From the Growth Mindset perspective, you are capable of change. This understanding gives you the freedom to choose to become the sort of person you want to be and lead the life you want to lead.

On the other hand, someone with a Fixed Mindset sees themselves as unchanging. Their choices are limited because they see people as fundamentally different. They can't become what someone else is, and so they must work out who they are and what their abilities will allow them do in life.

Fortunately, there is good evidence to show that we are capable of significant change, and this gives us the Rule of Choice. This rule holds that we not only have free will, but we also have the capacity to act on this free will to become who we want to be. We are not locked into, or out of, pathways in life based on any innate difference between us and anyone else.

Before we look at why we have choice, let's look at the negative Mindset Mover that sends the opposite message: categories.

Negative Mindset Mover: Categories

The idea of categories is a negative Mindset Mover that opposes choice. It is the idea that people are born different, and that we can be placed into different categories based on our genetics.

The belief that we are born with innate, unchangeable differences is highly restrictive. It means that our choices about the sort of person we can become, and the talents and abilities we can develop, are limited because of the way we were born. Essentially, this negative Mindset Mover restricts us by telling us we are limited in *where* we can grow.

We've all heard the saying, "We're all born different." No doubt, you've also heard that some people are "born" smart, musical or mathematical, or with some other gift or ability. We are naturally "cut out" for some roles, but not others. This negative Mindset Mover suggests that we are capable of growth, but are only capable of significant growth in a limited number of areas.

Many of us would have first heard of this negative Mindset Mover from our parents. For example, you may have been told that your older sister was artistic and your younger brother was more mathematical. Or you may have been told that since you took after your father, you were language oriented like him. Because of these differences, your sister was going to be an interior designer or artist, your older brother was going to be an engineer or computer programmer, and you were going to be a writer or journalist.

The idea of innate intelligence is, of course, one of the big categorisers. This negative Mindset Mover tells us that people are born with a certain amount of intelligence, and that those lucky enough to be born with more intelligence are more able and likely to become successful.

> Whenever you hear the idea that there are different types of people in the world, *and that our differences stem from the way we were born,* you are hearing a negative Mindset Mover that breaks the Rule of Choice.

There would, of course, be no problem with this worldview if it were true. The problem is that it's not true, and believing it to be true creates the Greatness Gap. This view separates you from those "with" the ability and, in doing so, pushes you towards a Fixed Mindset.

Multiple Intelligences

Psychologist Howard Gardner is the father of the Theory of Multiple Intelligences. His work has been widely applied in education, and it provides an excellent backdrop for a discussion about innate differences, as it combines both the perception of categories and our understanding of intelligence.

Prior to Gardner's work, the dominant theory was that of generalisable intelligence, or "g". The idea was that there exists a measurable and important general intelligence that's part of our genetic make-up. Simply, some people were born with a lot of "g", so were smarter, while others had less "g". But Gardner redefined intelligence in an incredibly powerful and practical way, describing it as *the ability to produce something valued by society*. Intelligence, in Gardner's view, wasn't an abstract general ability – it was something specific and practical.

Gardner also pointed out that any valid test of a person's proficiency in an intelligence should focus on *what the person can do*. He emphasised that intelligence isn't about what you are or what you were born with, it is about the actions you are capable of taking and what they produce.

Applying his definition of intelligence to various pursuits, hence the term "multiple intelligences", Gardner proposed that there are multiple ways through which an individual can create something valued by society, including
- Musical
- Mathematical

- Bodily/Kinesthetic
- Intrapersonal
- Interpersonal
- Linguistic
- Naturalistic
- Existential.

Using this definition, the people able to produce the things most valued by society have the greatest intelligences. Of course, many pursuits require an individual to apply more than one intelligence. Succeeding in business, for example, often requires well-developed mathematical, intrapersonal, interpersonal and linguistic intelligences. A dancer, on the other hand, might require a mix of well-developed musical, kinesthetic and interpersonal intelligences to interpret music and dance effectively as part of a company.

> Gardner's theory not only redefined intelligence, it proposed that intelligences are developed throughout our lives, rather than being fixed at birth.

Using Gardner's definition of intelligence – the ability to produce something valued by society – it's clear that the intelligence we are born with is not sufficient for adult performance. No child is born with intelligence sufficient to create something highly valued by society, so you've got to work at developing it.

What's more, you are capable of developing any, and all, of your intelligences. While you might be born with a preference for an intelligence, that intelligence is not well developed, and you are not restricted from developing your other intelligences. Your profile of intelligence, far from being a category you're destined to belong to all your life, provides multiple areas in which you can specialise.

Section 3.1: The Rule of Choice

While it is true that, as we look at the adults in the world, we can identify people with strengths in different intelligences, and in different combinations of intelligences, it is not true to say that this is because they were born that way. As Gardner (2011) states, "At any given moment, individuals differ for both genetic and experiential reasons in their respective profiles of intellectual strengths and weaknesses." What we see around us as adults is the result of *specialisation* – focused effort and development in certain areas – not the result of being born a "type".

Perhaps Gardner should have called his theory the Theory of Multiple Developable Intelligences.

Multiple Intelligences – Misunderstood

Consider the following scenario as an example of how we can misunderstand the nature of multiple intelligences:

> A child who is a few years old plays a simple rhythm on a drum. This ability seems amazing compared to her peers. Her mother, observing this, identifies her child as "being" musical. She tells people, "She's always loved musical things. She'll be a musician or grow up to do something in music for sure!"

The trouble with this evaluation is that the child is not displaying a *high degree* of musical intelligence. What the child has produced would not fit into Gardner's definition of intelligence, because the ability to produce a simple rhythm is not highly valued by society. It illustrates a level of intelligence that is easily exceeded by most adults and so, by Gardner's definition, the child is, in fact, displaying a low degree of musical intelligence.

I hear this sort of example frequently. Teachers and parents tend to incorrectly categorise children and make predictions about their adult strengths based on their current abilities and preferences.

The problems with this are:

You're not born intelligent. You develop your intelligences

By comparing the child to her peers, we falsely extrapolate that a difference now will be present later in life. Or we assume that because she is superior to her peers in this intelligence now she will be superior in the future.

The truth is that this child – and any child, for that matter – does not have particularly well-developed musical intelligence. She may be slightly better than some of her peers, but she's not good by any adult standard. In fact, in a short period of time, it's likely that most of her peers will develop their musical intelligence sufficiently to produce the same outcome.

To have a high degree of musical intelligence and produce music that is valued by society, the child must work on developing it. She will not get better by simply getting older – she's going to have to do the hard work. (We'll discuss what this sort of hard work looks like in the section on the Rule of Practice.)

Of course, it's not reasonable to expect a child of this young age to have a highly developed musical intelligence. It takes time and plenty of work to develop that ability, which is precisely the point!

You can change your strengths

We often mistakenly assume that a person's preference is an indication of "having" a certain intelligence. In the example above, the child may

Section 3.1: The Rule of Choice

have a preference for musical intelligence, so her mother assumes she is "musical". The problem with this is that we are assuming the child's profile of intelligences will always look the same: that her strength and preference will always be in music.

> Gardner points out that most "multiple intelligence tests" only assess a person's preference, and not their absolute ability, but it is the *absolute ability* that's important.

When we look at this child's behaviour, we are likely observing her preference only.

It is also entirely possible, and even desirable, that by working on developing all her intelligences, she can not only become proficient in her least-preferred intelligence, but also develop it to a level that's higher than any of her other intelligences. For example, this child might choose to pursue a career as a music journalist. To do this, she might need to develop her linguistic intelligence to a much higher level than her musical intelligence. This would completely change her intelligence profile, but not her preference.

> One might argue that the development of *all our intelligences* should be a major goal of our education system.

When we see a child with a preference, even a relative strength, for one intelligence, should our reaction be to nurture that ability? Or perhaps should we instead recognise that they need to spend more time developing their other intelligences?

East Versus West

It's interesting to note that the idea we are born with certain fixed intelligences is a uniquely Western interpretation of Gardner's work.

In China, the idea of multiple intelligences has gained great popularity. In the introduction to the 30th-anniversary edition of his book, *Frames of Mind* (Fontana Press, 1983), Gardner notes that there have been more than 2500 papers and 100 books written about multiple intelligences in China.

Gardner (2011) recounts a conversation he had with a Chinese journalist, who explained China's enormous interest in multiple intelligences this way: "In America, when people hear about [multiple intelligences], they think of their child. 'She may not be good in math, or in music, but she has wonderful interpersonal intelligence,' they declare. In China, these are simply eight areas we want our child to excel."

Positive Mindset Movers for the Rule of Choice

To create positive Mindset Movers, we must first acknowledge that people are born with different abilities. Then, we must recognise that the abilities we are born with aren't significant on an adult scale. To excel on an adult scale, we must work hard at developing those abilities.

We must help students recognise that their current strengths aren't destined to be their future strengths, and that they can specialise in other areas if they so choose. Being born with a natural tendency for numbers doesn't mean you can't learn to be exceptional with words.

We must also help children recognise that the people they see with strengths in certain areas have a backstory of specialisation. They didn't become good at something simply by getting older, they took action and put in the right sort of effort. In fact, they may have had entirely different strengths as children.

Section 3.1: The Rule of Choice

When we look around us, we see people with great capacity in music, maths, the arts and in each of Gardner's intelligences, but they were not always great. They were never destined to be that way. These people chose to develop their intelligences and abilities through a process of specialisation, and there is a backstory to how they became musical or mathematical.

By all means, encourage children to pursue their interests, even their strengths. But don't let them believe they should pursue them because they couldn't be good at anything else.

Remember, at its heart, the Growth Mindset gives us choice. We can choose to pursue our strengths, or we can choose to develop new ones.

> You can choose not to get good at something, but there's a big difference between not becoming good at something because you don't want to, and not becoming good at something because you don't believe that you can.

Racing Cars and Driving Skills

Let me share an analogy with you, one that I feel helps us better understand the role of innate difference. It will also pave the way for our discussion about the Truths of Practice, Effort and Unlimited Growth.

The analogy originally comes from physician and psychologist Edward de Bono. De Bono recognises that we are all born different. He suggests your innate abilities are like the car you drive. We are all born with a certain make and model, and you don't get to upgrade. Some of us are lucky enough to be born with a Ferrari, while others must make do with a Mini – or anything in between.

However, de Bono also asserts that your success in life is more closely related to how well you learn to drive.

Let's put this analogy into context. Imagine me, born with a Ferrari, next to racing-car driver Nigel Mansell, born with a Mini. We line up on a drag track. The light goes green. Who's going to win?

In my Ferrari, I'm going to win that race every day of the week. Providing I have the most basic of driving skills – being able to hold the steering wheel straight and knowing which pedal is the accelerator – I will win that race. On easy tasks, natural ability will win. But life isn't an easy task.

Now, imagine Mansell and I racing on a rally track – something full of challenges and changing terrain. Who do you think would win that race? I'm likely to crash out at the first significant challenge. Mansell, with his superior learnt skills, would fly past me to win the race.

Life is more like a rally track. There are corners, changing surfaces, pot holes and traffic; a whole host of challenges. What's more, these challenges change all the time. The challenges at the end of the race may not have been there at the start.

Let's bring this analogy closer to home.

Have you ever known someone at school who you might call a "lazy A student"? These are the kids born with a Ferrari, born with natural ability, but the tasks we ask them to do at school are easy – compared to what we would expect of them as highly successful adults performing complex tasks in a changing world.

Section 3.1: The Rule of Choice

These lazy A students cruise through school, but at some point, the track rises to meet them. Perhaps it will be at one of those key transition periods – primary to secondary school, the middle years to senior school, Year 12 to university – but at that point, when things start getting difficult, these students often crash out of the race.

On the other hand, you might have known a student who was born with a scooter. This student never finds the work easy, but learns how to work hard. They don't ask, "What's the answer?" They ask, "How do I work out the answer? What do I have to do to understand this?"

When you reflect on the characteristically successful people you know, those in the public eye and those closer to home, do you think most of them were born with Ferraris? Or do you think they learnt to become good drivers?

My assertion is that we are all born different, but those innate differences aren't enough to see us thrive in the volatile, uncertain, complex and ambiguous world we find ourselves in as adults. Perhaps it was at some point, but not so any more. Furthermore, the influence of your learnt intelligence on your real-life success far outstrips that of your innate intelligence. If we are to thrive in this world, we need to learn new driving skills.

SECTION 3.2
The Rule of Practice

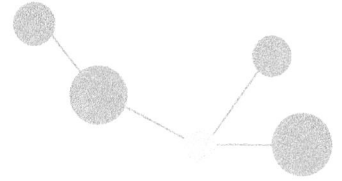

The Rule of Practice states that in order to increase your talents and abilities, you have to practice!

The rule holds that your talents and abilities are developed through practice, and only through practice. Significant improvement only occurs through the accumulation of many hours of practice over a long period of time, and those who practice effectively for the greatest number of hours (approximately) will develop the greatest abilities.

The result of the Rule of Practice is a common backstory to every achievement; a backstory of many hundreds of hours of focused, and often unnoticed, practice.

Everyone can engage in the sort of practice that results in increased talents and abilities. Furthermore, because of the Rule of Choice, you can practice in any domain and increase your relevant abilities in that domain.

Negative Mindset Movers: When Practice Doesn't Work

The Rule of Practice is often undermined by our own lived experiences, where we may have "learnt" that practice doesn't always work.

There are several ways this negative Mindset Mover manifests itself:

Limited progress

"No matter how hard I try, I've never been any good at that."

We practice and practice, but to little or no avail. We've reached a Performance Plateau and can't break through. What's worse is that we can see it's possible to be better. There are plenty of other people better than us, but we don't seem to "have it in us" to significantly improve.

Each time we do not see increases in our abilities due to what we call "practice", it's easy to believe that those abilities *cannot* change.

Unequal progress

"I could practice all day and not get that. But Jimmy just picks it up so easily!"

We may have experienced a situation where practice seems unequal. Some people appear to get more results out of their practice than others. We put in the same amount of practice as everyone else, but others seem to learn quicker!

Alternatively, we might be the one learning more rapidly, so we assume that we are naturally better than others.

Different rates of improvement can create the belief that practice pays off for some people more than it does for others.

No progress

"I can't do that no matter what."

Section 3.2: The Rule of Practice

Sometimes we hear people say, "I've never been able to do that." But if you dig deeper and ask how much practice they've put in, we discover that they have resigned themselves to the fact they can't do it, and so do nothing about getting better. They engage in no practice at all, and yet are surprised that they haven't progressed.

Anders Ericsson points out that this often happens after we have been categorised by someone as "not" being something, breaking the Rule of Choice.

> Once we're told we "can't" do something, we stop "wasting our time" in trying. We stop practicing, and remove any chance of getting better.

When our experience is that we don't change, it creates the belief that we *can't* change. The lack of action to facilitate change is ignored, and not knowing how to change is interpreted as not being able to change.

Practicing in the Right Place

Not All Hours Are Equal

The experiences above can lead to the conclusion that practice doesn't always pay off. Fortunately, that conclusion is incorrect – if you're doing the right sort of practice.

Reaching a Performance Plateau merely reflects a lack of understanding of how to continue to grow, not an inability to grow. Simply because two people practice together does not mean they are doing the same thing, nor that they started at the same level. And it's hardly surprising that if you don't take action, and don't practice at all, you're not going to get better.

> The number of hours you spend practicing *is* directly related to how much you improve. But it's not only the hours that count: it's *where* you spend those hours and *what you do* during those hours – in other words, *how* you practice – that makes all the difference.

Let's start with "where".

Practicing in the Right Place

To practice in the right place doesn't mean you must sit in a quiet room, or go to the right gym, school or centre – although all these things can be important. It refers to where you are practicing in relation to your current abilities.

When we look closely at the way most people practice, they tend to practice things they can already do. Practice is often considered to mean repetition or rehearsal. While this sort of practice may lead to increased reliability, it does not create improvements in ability.

To help us understand the effects of different sorts of practice, let's return to the Performance Plateau.

The Performance Plateau

As we discussed in Section 1, when trying new things, most people improve and experience growth *up to a point*. After this point, further progress becomes more difficult and may seem impossible. This is the Performance Plateau, an apparent ceiling to our standard of performance.

Section 3.2: The Rule of Practice

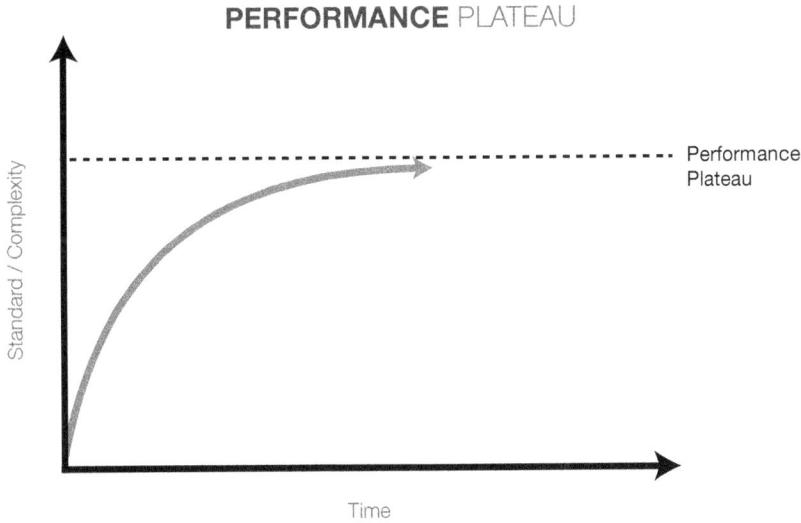

Notice that the vertical axis of the Performance Plateau relates to the difficulty of a task. We are talking about increasing the standards or complexity of what we're able to do.

> It's not simply about being able to do more things – it's about being able to do things that are *more difficult.*

Easy New? Or Hard New?

Our everyday experience tells us that not everything we try for the first time is difficult. Sometimes we try a new task and master it quickly and easily. We often inaccurately describe this accumulation of new abilities as growth.

The reality is that not all new tasks are equal. There are two basic categories when it comes to learning new things:

1. Easy things we haven't done yet.
2. Hard things we haven't done yet.

Easy Things We Haven't Done Yet

As the name suggests, "easy things we haven't done yet" come readily to us. We try something new and see progress without much effort.

Drawing on our racing car analogy, it's like driving on a new, yet straightforward racetrack. It's an easy track, similar to every other track you've driven. Sure, you might need to drive it a few times to become familiar with the specifics of it, but you've already got the required driving skills. You don't need to become a more skilful driver to master this new racetrack.

In this case, new is *different*, not *difficult*. You've learnt to do *more* things, but you haven't learnt to do a more *difficult* thing.

We are regularly confronted with new problems that are "easy things we haven't done yet". For example, when we learn to follow a new recipe, we are learning how to cook more things, but we probably aren't learning to be a better cook.

> We quickly master "easy things we haven't done yet" by drawing on our existing knowledge and behaviours. We may imagine we are progressing, but in reality we are simply doing more. We are not doing anything *more difficult*.

Section 3.2: The Rule of Practice

Hard Things You Haven't Done Yet

Of course, not all new tasks are easy. Some are difficult. We struggle with them, often experiencing mistakes and failure, and do not see anything that looks like progress. "Hard things we haven't done yet" are difficult because we can't solve them with our current behaviours. To master this kind of task, we must develop new skills.

Drawing again on our racing car analogy, learning a "hard thing you haven't done yet" is like driving on a new track, but this time the track presents something difficult, something you haven't encountered before. We can't rely solely on our existing skills. Perhaps there's a series of sharp corners at the bottom of a hill, unlike anything you've had to deal with before. Chances are, the first time around you'll make a mistake and crash. Before you can master this new track, you need to learn new driving skills.

> When we work on mastering "hard things we haven't done yet", we are not simply learning to do more, we are learning to do *better*.

Negative Mindset Mover: Easy Things We Haven't Done Yet

If we spend lots of time focusing on learning "easy things we haven't done yet", we can come to believe that learning, or at least some areas of learning, is easy. So, when we inevitably encounter something difficult, causing us to struggle and make mistakes, we incorrectly believe we've encountered some sort of limit – a Performance Plateau. Learning to recognise the difference between *learning to do more* and *learning to do better* is critical in developing a Growth Mindset, and helping to guide our growth.

To help us understand the difference between doing more and doing better, it's useful to look again at our Performance Plateau, and divide it into three zones: our Comfort Zone, our Performance Zone and our Learning Zone.

PERFORMANCE PLATEAU

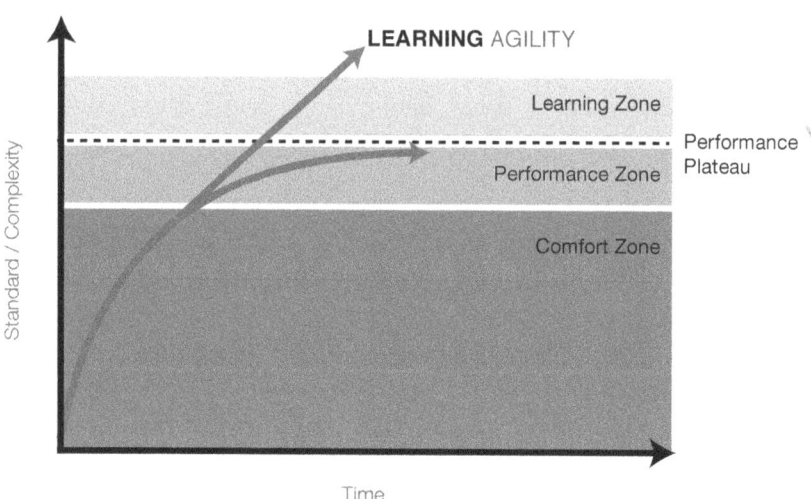

Comfort Zone

Your Comfort Zone contains tasks you find *easy*: things you've already done and easy things you haven't done yet. When we work in our Comfort Zone, we use our current, established behaviours to complete tasks at a level we've previously mastered.

> Think of your Comfort Zone as the "Zone of More", rather than the "Zone of Better".

It's where you either do the things you know you can already do (because you've done them before), or you learn to do things that come easily to you. It's like moving sideways: increasing breadth, not moving up and increasing depth.

When we do things that are in our Comfort Zone, we don't *stretch* ourselves, we simply *apply* ourselves by utilising well-established skills. Working at this level usually takes little real effort or concentration.

Section 3.2: The Rule of Practice

We cannot get better and master more difficult things by working in our Comfort Zone. Breaking through the Performance Plateau is about mastering *more difficult* things, raising your abilities to a new and higher level. So, working in your Comfort Zone, at a level you've previously mastered, cannot get you past your Performance Plateau to a new, or higher, level of working.

Performance Zone

Sitting just below the level of our Performance Plateau is our Performance Zone. This is our best work, our highest standard, and consists of the most difficult work we can reliably do. It requires us to use not only our existing knowledge, but also our most well-developed existing behaviours. When we are in our Performance Zone, we do our (current) best.

There are times when we want to be in our Performance Zone, such as in performance and high-stakes situations where we need to produce our most reliable, high-quality work. Test situations, high-stakes situations where there are serious consequences for mistakes and some elements of our day-to-day work life are all examples of times when it's important to be in our Performance Zone.

When we work in our Performance Zone, our energy and concentration levels are typically high. The Performance Zone is characterised by our highest level of mastery: it is where we display our best work.

The trouble with being in the Performance Zone is that, like the Comfort Zone, we repeat existing behaviours – albeit our most well-developed ones. Doing the same thing, or working at the same level, no matter how difficult it might be, does not help you learn how to do something more difficult.

Staying in your Performance Zone might make you more reliable at performing the task, but it does not take you to a higher level. For example, playing a piece of music repeatedly may make you better at performing that piece of music, but you won't learn how to master the chords in a more difficult piece. You do not grow.

The Performance Zone is seductive. We know our best; it's reliable. We often look good doing our best. People employ us to do our best. But we also know that if we push ourselves beyond our best, the result may be worse than our best!

The Learning Zone

The Learning Zone lies just beyond the Performance Zone. In this zone, we attempt to do better than our best, and ironically it involves a decrease in the standard of our performance.

If you've ever tried to learn how to touch type, you'll know this feeling. Chances are you were a proficient "hunt-and-peck" typist. You'd reached a Performance Plateau with your two-finger typing – a maximum number of words per minute that was "good enough", perhaps as many as 20 words per minute – but you wanted to get better, so you tried to touch type using all 10 fingers.

As you tried to learn to use all 10 fingers, your typing speed plummeted. You went from 20 words per minutes to 10, or even less, and your error rate skyrocketed. You felt as though you'd be better off staying with two fingers! So, you went back to your old, reliable, hunt-and-peck method, sticking to a safe 20 words per minute. The realm of 40-plus words a minute seemed unreachable.

> Pushing ourselves beyond our best – trying something harder, or trying to do better than our best – results in a temporary *decrease* in standards.

Section 3.2: The Rule of Practice

In the face of this decrease, our natural tendency is to retreat to the Performance Zone, where we can get our best results. But if we want to improve, if we want to master more difficult things, beyond our (current) best is exactly where we must go.

Practice in the Right Place: Improving Ability

If our goal is to improve our ability, then we need to practice in the Learning Zone. Spending time in our Comfort Zone may expand our abilities, but it will not improve them. Similarly, we might become more reliable by spending time rehearsing in our Performance Zone, but we do not get better. While there are times when expanding our abilities or improving our reliability are important, ultimately, it is time spent in the Learning Zone that will help us get better.

Our challenge is that to improve, we must first get worse. Stretching ourselves beyond our current abilities results in mistakes, and usually a decrease in performance. But we must recognise that these mistakes do not define the limit of our abilities, as someone with a Fixed Mindset would see them. Rather, mistakes are our signposts to future learning, guiding us towards our future growth.

The Learning Zone is the "where" we need to learn and is a critical part of the Rule of Practice. Understanding the role of mistakes in learning is our first step in understanding the "how" of the Rule of Practice.

Practicing in the Right Way

To practice in the right way means that you actively look for the pathway towards a higher level of performance. Your Growth Mindset gives you the understanding that the pathway exists, and entering your Learning Zone represents your first steps along that path. But what's next? In which direction does that path lead? Fortunately, the pathway to improved performance is signposted for us.

Mistakes and Other Signposts for Learning

There is a common misnomer that says, "Every mistake you make is progress." This is not true, as mistakes themselves do not represent progress. In fact, every mistake indicates of a lack of progress, and merely signposts the way forward. It's how you respond to the mistake, and the actions you take, that represent progress.

Currently, there is a lot of excitement about the role mistakes play in learning. Certainly, mistakes are one way of knowing that you're in the Learning Zone – you're stretching yourself by trying something that's slightly beyond your current abilities. But a mistake does more than just tell you you're in your Learning Zone. It also signposts where you need to direct your attention for learning, pointing the way toward further growth. If you've got something wrong, then that's something you need to learn.

Eduardo Briceno (2015), co-founder of Mindset Works, points out that not all mistakes are equal, and that some have higher learning potential than others. While all mistakes – including sloppy mistakes, high-stakes mistakes and the accidental mistakes of "aha" moments – are useful in signposting what we need to learn, the highest learning potential comes from "stretch" mistakes, which occur when we deliberately push ourselves into our Learning Zone. We expect these mistakes to happen, and we are ready for them. In anticipation of their occurrence, we explicitly pay attention to what they tell us about our learning needs.

But with so much focus on mistakes, we have lost sight of other signposts for learning. Other signals that, like mistakes, point out the direction for future growth. In fact, it's a mistake to think that mistakes are the only signposts that can guide our learning.

Mistakes are often easy to recognise, so they make for useful markers. But they aren't the only way to guide our future learning. Here are six other important signposts for future learning:

Section 3.2: The Rule of Practice

Expert guidance

"An expert is a person who has made all the mistakes that can be made in a very narrow field." – Niels Bohr

An expert is someone who not only has made mistakes, but also has learnt from them and knows how to correct or avoid them. They have been down this path before, and so they are excellent signposts to guide your learning.

Anders Ericsson points out that what he calls the "gold standard of practice" – Deliberate Practice – requires an expert guide. This is someone who knows the path towards greater achievement, has walked it themselves and is able to guide you along that same path, predicting and correcting your missteps along the way.

A problem

"If I had an hour to solve a problem, I'd spend 55 minutes thinking about the problem and five minutes thinking about solutions." – Albert Einstein

Before a mistake becomes a mistake, it's a problem that you don't know the answer to. When we recognise a problem, we recognise a learning opportunity. Identifying what that problem is and applying our existing understanding will either yield a solution, which is the next step on our learning journey, or lead to a mistake that we can use to guide our learning.

Inconsistencies or incongruences

"It would be so nice if things made sense for a change." – Lewis Carroll, *Alice's Adventures in Wonderland*

Sometimes things don't seem to make sense. One set of data doesn't match another set of data. The solution to a problem when approached from one direction may change when we approach the problem from a different direction. Recognising and analysing these inconsistencies acts as a signpost for where our future learning lies.

Albert Einstein was famous for using these sorts of signposts for future learning. He conducted "thought experiments", where he imagined what it would be like to ride along with a beam of light. But in doing so, he realised his idea didn't make sense. The wave that made up light wouldn't work if you were travelling at the same speed. From this and similar thought experiments, he followed a learning path that led him to develop the theories of special and general relativity.

Missing the mark

"Missing the mark is one of the ways in which we learn to hit the target." – Eric Butterworth

Like a bullseye on a target, some goals have finite measures. With these goals, you know when you've hit the target. Falling short of a goal isn't necessarily a failure, but it does highlight where your pathway for future learning lies. This signpost points you towards your goal, indicating where you need to make adjustments to close that gap in your knowledge or skills.

Continuous improvement

"The enemy of the 'best' is often the 'good'." – Stephen Covey

Not everything has a finite end state. Many things can be continually improved. Simply asking, "How could this be done better?" or, "How might we further refine/extend/build upon this?", even when what you're doing is being done well, can reveal areas for further development.

Section 3.2: The Rule of Practice

The signpost for future learning points in the direction of continuous improvement.

Alternatives

"We may have a perfectly adequate way of doing something, but that does not mean there cannot be a better way. So we set out to find an alternative way. This is the basis of any improvement that is not fault correction or problem solving." – Edward de Bono

The search for alternatives, even when the current solution is working, can reveal new learning opportunities. This is not about refining a current solution, it's about finding an entirely new one. Simply asking, "How else might this be done?" can open a whole new world of possibilities.

Importantly, we must recognise that all the above examples are just *signposts* for future learning, and not actual learning. Signposts point the way, but it is taking action to correct them that results in learning. To learn and improve, we must *recognise* the signposts, *understand* what they tell us and *act* on them effectively.

How to Make Use of a Signpost

On its own, these signposts have no value. The value and learning potential come from the way we act on the signpost. To achieve learning, and act on these signposts effectively, we must follow Anders Ericsson's 3 Fs:

- Focus: We must pay attention, and know what we are paying attention to, to know what the signpost is telling us.
- Feedback: We must gather feedback so we can tell where our current performance is in relation to our goal.
- Fix It: We must take action to follow the signpost, correct our mistake and perform at the higher level.

Focus

When we are in our Learning Zone, we expect to see signposts for future learning. We pay attention to the mistakes, the shortfalls, the opportunities to improve and the other signposts mentioned above.

To do this, we first need to have a clear understanding of what we are trying to achieve: our desired end state or goal. This is why the use of exemplars, experts, clear rubrics, key performance indicators and well-defined goals are so important. They give us a clear understanding of what we are trying to achieve.

Without this focused attention to what we are trying to achieve, we are unable to recognise our signposts. We are simply "working hard" and "doing our best", without a way of knowing where our hard work should be taking us, or what our best should look like.

Feedback

A signpost for future learning is of no use to us if we don't know which way it's pointing. To work out where our signposts are pointing, we need to compare our current state with our desired goals. We not only need to know where we are going, but also where we are now. To do this, we need feedback.

Feedback requires us to have accurate knowledge of our current state compared to our goal. We must be able to extract the information that will help guide our actions in getting us from one state to the other, so that we can make a plan of action.

Without the ability to compare, draw a path between desired and actual states, and plan our actions, we are lost. All we know is that we are not where we are meant to be. The signpost is there, but we don't know which way it's pointing. This is when an expert, someone who's experienced it before, is so helpful in guiding our learning. An expert can discern the error and the course of action required to correct it. In the absence of an expert, we need to have clear and helpful criteria about our current and goal states, as well as strategies to move from one to the other.

This is also why our Learning Zone is *just* beyond our current abilities. When the goal is too far away from our current performance, it is difficult, or even impossible, to work out a path between the two.

Fix It

Up until this point, learning has not taken place. All that has happened is we've identified a signpost for learning, and worked out the direction in which it is pointing. For a learning opportunity to become actual learning, you must take action to fix the mistake. Simply knowing you're not where you want to be, and thinking you know the way forward, is not enough. For learning to have taken place, you need to have fixed the mistake and changed your behaviour.

Having identified a possible course of action, you must modify your actions and test your theory. The result will either be that your plan of action is accurate and you arrive at your goal, or that your plan of action is incorrect, in which case you need to detect and act upon the new signposts for future learning.

> Learning is not about making mistakes. Learning is about detecting signposts for learning. It is about understanding what these signposts tell us, and acting upon that so we can modify our actions, learn and grow.

Virtuous Practice

The sort of practice that follows the 3 Fs, and occurs in your Learning Zone, is what I refer to as Virtuous Practice. This captures the fact that, unlike other forms of practice, it has the virtue of leading to growth in your abilities. By increasing your abilities, it allows you to do more difficult things, not simply more of the easy things you haven't done yet. Virtuous Practice encompasses what Ericsson calls Deliberate Practice and Purposeful Practice.

As previously mentioned, Ericsson refers to Deliberate Practice as the "gold standard of practice", not only because it utilises the 3 Fs, but also that it is guided by an expert. This expert has experienced the learning journey before, usually along with many others who have taken a similar journey, so the path to expertise is well known. The expert can guide your next steps, help you identify where signposts exist and the direction they are pointing, and provide you with proven strategies to continue to improve.

Purposeful Practice, on the other hand, follows the 3 Fs but has no clear path to future growth. It is not a path that has been previously travelled by many experts, as in Deliberate Practice, and often involves "breaking new ground" or "trail blazing". Purposeful Practice is required in any new field, including at the very edge of human performance, where new standards are being set according to the Rule of Unlimited Growth, which we will discuss later.

You can think of the difference between Deliberate and Virtuous Practice like this. With Deliberate Practice, you make use of an expert who has a road map. The expert has travelled the road before, so they know what to expect and what's required at each stage of the journey. The road to improvement is a well-worn one and you are travelling with a guide. Deliberate Practice is why programs such as the Suzuki method of music training work so well. It is also the reason why the student Daniel, in *The Karate Kid*, was made to "wax on, wax off". The master knew that this was the next step along the path towards mastering specific karate skills.

Section 3.2: The Rule of Practice

Typically, Deliberate Practice is more relevant to areas where there are well-defined standards of expertise, and where a good number of people who could be considered experts have become the teachers. Areas such as playing classical violin, chess or ballet are good examples.

With Purposeful Practice, there is no existing road map, and no one to tell you what you need to do next. You must create the map for yourself. Each time you venture into your Learning Zone, you map out new territory. Because it is new territory, there are likely to be more missteps and progress will be slower.

Purposeful Practice is more relevant to areas that are less well defined. The art of writing and business are good examples. There are people out there who have done a good job before and can guide you, but you're not doing exactly what they did. Your path may be similar in some respects, but different overall.

> Virtuous Practice is at the heart of the Rule of Practice. It involves not only practicing in the right place – your Learning Zone – but also in the right way – with the 3 Fs. This sort of practice leads to growth and, as we'll see when we look at the Rule of Unlimited Growth, there is no point at which this sort of practice does not result in further growth.

Deliberate Practice, if it's available to you, will be faster, but any form of Virtuous Practice will lead to improvement.

Virtuous Practice and Your Potential

Virtuous Practice allows you to do things you could not do before. It literally extends your abilities. In terms of our Performance Plateau, it "raises the bar", making things possible that were not possible before. So, as we return to our Learning Agility diagram, we see that by applying our Growth Mindset to Virtuous Practice we build our potential.

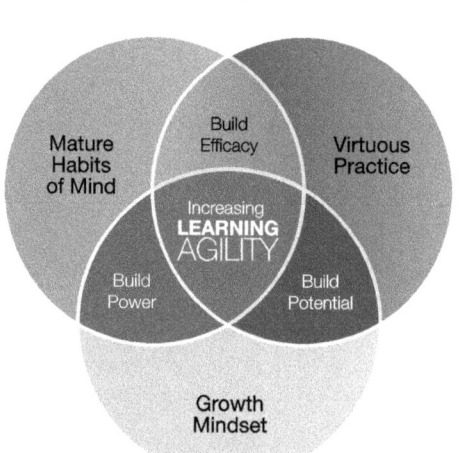

As Anders Ericsson and Robert Pool (2016) put it, "Learning isn't a way of reaching your potential, it's a way of building it."

Naive Practice: A Negative Mindset Mover

Unfortunately, often when people say they are practicing, they are actually engaging in what is called Naive Practice. Naive Practice lacks one or more of the key characteristics of Virtuous Practice, as it is either conducted in the wrong "place" or the wrong "way".

When someone routinely engages in Naive Practice, they create the negative Mindset Movers mentioned at the start of this section. Their lack of progress is a result of one of the following:
- Not stretching themselves into their Learning Zone.
- Not recognising the signposts for learning.
- Not gathering feedback and formulating a plan for future action.
- Not acting on that plan to achieve the new higher standard.

Section 3.2: The Rule of Practice

When someone spends time and energy engaged in Naive Practice, they fail to grow. Faced with this lack of growth, the person mistakes their lack of understanding of how to grow with an inability to grow. This negative Mindset Mover leads them to the conclusion that they are unable to change – at least in this area – and they are pushed towards the Low-Growth end of the Mindset Continuum.

Learning to identify the difference between Naive and Virtuous Practice is essential. When engaging in Virtuous Practice, you experience the underlying reality of the Growth Mindset: that you are capable of growth. This experience acts as a positive Mindset Mover, allowing you to engage in the Rule of Practice and develop your talents and abilities.

NAIVE VS VIRTUOUS PRACTICE

Reflect on your current goals and your practices towards achieving them. Do you tend to engage in Naive Practice, or Virtuous Practice?

	Naive Practice	Virtuous Practice
Nature of Goals	Big/General	Small/Specific
Location of Goals	Comfort Zone Possibly "easy things you haven't done yet." Well outside your Performance Zone; too long term.	Learning Zone Building on and extending existing capacities. Slightly better than you current best.
Process for Achieving Goals	Vague Working hard. Concentrating. Doing a course.	Specific Opportunity for 3Fs: • Focus • Feedback • Fix It
Type of Effort	Performance or Ineffective Effort	Effective Effort
Types of Mistakes	Low Learning Potential High-Stakes Mistakes: to be avoided due undesirable consequences. Sloppy Mistakes: due to carelessness not applying previous learning.	High Learning Potential Provide information about performance and guide action for future development.

	Naive Practice	Virtuous Practice
Success Criteria	**Ambiguous** Terms like: "better" or "more". Often defined in terms of outcomes (e.g. greater sales) rather than personal skills and behaviours.	**Clear** Usually defined in terms of personal actions. New mental models, and ways of working, are created as a result.
Support	**Resources** Support is likely to be limited to time and resources.	**Expertise** Support is through guidance of an expert, coach or mentor. Where access to expert, coach or mentor isn't available opportunities to learn from expert performance are provided.

Download this infographic in full size from
www.jamesanderson.com.au/p/TheAgileLearnerDownloads/

How Much Practice Do You Need?

In his book *Outliers* (Little, Brown and Company, 2008), Malcolm Gladwell popularised the "10 000-Hour Rule". Gladwell asserts that it takes about 10 000 hours of Deliberate Practice to reach a world-class standard. In deriving this rule, Gladwell drew on the work of Ericsson, as well as his own research.

Ericsson has since disputed 10 000 hours as a *rule*. He points out that in fields that are less highly developed, it may take less than 10 000 hours to become world class. Conversely, in highly developed fields, Ericsson says it may take much longer to get to a world-class standard, and notes that many top performers continue to practice and develop their talents all their lives, significantly exceeding 10 000 hours.

Section 3.2: The Rule of Practice

Ericsson also highlights that some of the hours Gladwell and others may have counted as practice may not have been spent in Virtuous Practice. Hours spent performing, where the goal is delivering the best-possible performance, is not the same as an hour spent in Virtuous Practice, where you deliberately stretch yourself and focus on the development of new talents and abilities. As Eduardo Briceno (2015) pointed out, the stretch mistakes you make as you deliberately put yourself into your Learning Zone have a higher learning potential than the high-stakes mistakes that may occur in performance situations.

Furthermore, Gladwell used The Beatles as an example of the 10 000-Hour Rule, citing widespread public appeal and record sales as evidence of their expertise. It's important to note that the outcome of Virtuous Practice is the accumulation of new talents and abilities. This is not necessarily the same as fame, public recognition, fortune or achieving a competitive goal – something we'll explore in Section 4 of this book. It may be that being extremely good at something makes you rich and famous, but the two are not interdependent.

But what is clear about Virtuous Practice is that
1. the more hours you spend engaged in the right sort of practice, the better you'll get
2. improvement doesn't happen overnight. Becoming significantly better requires the accumulation of many hours of practice
3. becoming world class often requires many thousands of hours of practice, which may span 10 years or more.

In short, no one becomes very good quickly. Improvement takes time.

The result of all this time spent in Virtuous Practice is the creation of a backstory.

Achievements and the Importance of Backstories

Achievements are easy to recognise. We know when a goal has been reached, a victory won, a challenge overcome or a new skill demonstrated. The problem has been solved. The champion stands on the podium. The previously impossible has become a reality, and talent has been demonstrated. These moments are a time for celebration. We tell the world what has been achieved. Our schools and communities are quick to celebrate these sorts of achievements, and rightly so. We should celebrate achievements and growth, but what are we *really* celebrating?

As we've demonstrated, significant achievements are the result of a long history of practice. New skills, abilities and talents are developed through the slow accumulation of many hours of practice, and these lead us to have the ability to accomplish something. What we tend to highlight in our celebrations, though, is the accomplishment, the end point of all that hard work. But in focusing our attention on the end point, the critical importance of the backstory can be lost.

> The problem is that the achievement is public, but the backstory remains private.

The hours and hours of hard work, spent quietly accumulating new abilities, occur outside of the public eye. Only the individual, and those closest to them, really know what goes on behind the scenes. No one notices you as you build your backstory. The recognition only comes when that backstory results in an achievement being reached.

For people with a Fixed Mindset, one of the reasons why the Greatness Gap exists is because they tend not to notice people going across it. For them, there is no path, no backstory, across the Greatness Gap. They have never paid attention to the person who was "becoming talented", and only recognise those who have achieved milestones, assuming they succeeded because they'd always had that ability. *Being* appears to come before *doing*.

Section 3.2: The Rule of Practice

When the backstory of an achievement is detached from the achievement, or hidden from us, it gives the appearance that the Rule of Practice can be broken. This is an extremely powerful negative Mindset Mover. At best, it leaves us with the impression that some people don't have to practice as much as others. At worst, it tells us that to have talents and abilities, you must be born with them. Unfortunately, this notion is becoming increasingly prevalent in a world of instant news and overnight success stories.

Reflect for a moment on how achievements are often portrayed in the media. The first time we hear about someone is the day they achieve something. All the focus is on the moment, on what they have achieved, and the years of hard work that led to it are either glossed over, or omitted altogether. We aren't interested in the thousands of hours of quiet, private, unrewarded practice and effort – we are interested in the moment all those hours amount to.

Consider, for example, the image of a person standing on top of Mount Everest. The moment we celebrate, the picture in our minds, is the person standing on the summit. But standing on top of Mount Everest isn't the real achievement, it is simply the evidence of it. The real achievement is climbing to the top!

The person standing on top of Mount Everest doesn't refer to themselves as a mountain "stander-on-top-of-er", they are a mountain climber. But for most of us, the focus is almost always on the fact that the summit has been reached, not on the climb to the top.

> To be a Growth Mindset teacher is, in many ways, about backstories.

It's about connecting a person's backstory to their achievement. It's about valuing how far students have come as much as – or more than –

where they have come to. It's about valuing what students are doing as they build their own backstories. And, essentially, it's about teaching students how to more effectively engage in and build their own backstories.

As real estate investor Kent Clothier so aptly put it, "The overnight part of the overnight success is just the sudden recognition of years of hard work." As Growth Mindset teachers, we create powerful, positive Mindset Movers when we recognise and value the backstory of achievements – backstories that contain long hours of quiet, focused practice and the slow development of talents. In doing so, we reinforce the Rule of Practice and develop Growth Mindsets.

Negative Mindset Movers: Achievement in the Absence of Backstory

Unfortunately, the recognition and reward systems in schools often overemphasise the accomplishment at the expense of the backstory. We focus on what students have done, rather than the backstory of what they did. When we do this, we risk detaching the backstory from the achievement and generating negative Mindset Movers.

Of course, as educators we know that the hard work is important. The time and effort – the backstory – that led to the achievement is what counts. But when we fail to make that connection clear to students, we create the illusion of the Greatness Gap, and in doing so contribute to a Fixed Mindset.

Think of the way awards are traditionally given in schools. They are for the students who can do the most, the ones who have achieved the highest. We stand them on stage and read out their accomplishments. To the students in the audience, it may appear as though those peers are simply better than the rest, able to do something the other students cannot, simply because they were born that way. The students are given little or no sense of how their peers' achievements were reached, and the Greatness Gap appears.

Traditional awards hide the hours of practice that go into reaching an achievement. We want all students to eventually reach the standards that are being celebrated, in whatever field they are pursuing. So why do we only show students the destination and not the way to get there?

We need to use these opportunities to not only celebrate students' achievements, but to signpost the common backstory of effort and growth for other students to accomplish their goals. Asking students to aspire to these sorts of results without highlighting how to achieve them is unreasonable.

One school I worked with many years ago recognised this problem and developed a fabulous solution. The school had a long tradition of recognising students for significant achievements, either academic achievements or relating to other areas of the school or community. These students were traditionally recognised at school assemblies, and their name, photo and achievement would be placed on the wall along with previous high achievers. This tradition spanned more than 100 years.

To students in the assembly hall, all they saw were students who had achieved. You can imagine a student pondering all the amazing students who had come to the school before them. The students were on the wall because they were amazing people, which explained why they could do such amazing things. It would take someone who already had a highly Growth-Oriented Mindset to ask how so many ordinary people had become extraordinary. But for most students, the display simply reinforced the Greatness Gap. They could not imagine how normal students such as themselves could possibly achieve such things.

The school recognised that celebrating achievements without highlighting the backstory that led to them created the Greatness Gap in the minds of many students. The school's solution was to attach the behaviours that led to the achievement to every award. Under each achievement was a list of the Habits of Mind that the students had engaged in to reach that achievement. Now, as students ponder all those diverse achievements, they not only see the achievements, but also a common set of behaviours that led to them.

What this school did was draw attention to the importance of the backstory in every achievement, as well as highlighting some of the behaviours that enabled these students to reach their achievements. This simple strategy emphasised the Rule of Practice (and pointed towards the Rule of Effort, which we'll discuss in the next section), and asserted that it's not *who you are* that matters, it's *what you do* that counts!

Negative Mindset Mover: The Myth of the Natural

Perhaps one of the most powerful negative Mindset Movers that breaks the Rule of Practice is the myth of "the natural". This is the person who does not have to practice for their abilities or, at the very least, needs to practice much less than other people. When we see people who we believe have natural abilities, we immediately create the Greatness Gap. These people are simply different to us, and we can't expect to be like them because we weren't born like them.

Good Will Hunting exemplifies this myth perfectly. In this movie, Matt Damon plays the layabout genius Will Hunting. He has exceptional mathematical abilities, which, "for someone who divides their time fairly evenly between batting cages and bars", are not necessary for his life. His abilities are portrayed almost as an affliction, a burden he has no control over. By comparison, as Minnie Driver's character points out, "There are really smart people here at Harvard, and even they have to study ... because this stuff is really hard."

To explain "how his mind works", Hunting says: "When Beethoven looked at a piano, it just made sense to him. He could just play ... I couldn't paint you a picture, I probably couldn't hit the ball out of Fenway, and I can't play the piano ... but when it came to stuff like (maths), I could always just play."

This myth is, perhaps, the ultimate representation of the Greatness Gap. It suggests that some people acquire a special ability with little or no effort, and that this ability is out of their control. They have it whether they want it or not. According to this myth, being exceptional is the result of some sort of cosmic lottery. Not only does the myth of the natural create the Greatness Gap and the Fixed Mindset, it robs "the natural" of what they deserve credit for: their backstory.

Mozart and Other Prodigies

I am not debating the existence of extraordinary abilities, as there is no doubt that the world is full of exceptional performers. This myth is not about the existence of extraordinary abilities, it's about *how* these abilities are acquired.

Our challenge with the myth of prodigies is that they seem to take so much less time to reach their amazing standards than anyone else. In the ultimate version of the myth, they take no time at all. It's as if they were born with fully fledged, exceptional adult abilities. How can these abilities be acquired with so little effort?

The short answer is that they aren't. The myth of the natural can be explained using the same method we used to explain the myth of innate differences: measuring sticks and backstories.

Measuring Sticks

Child "prodigies" are exceptional for their age. When *compared to other, similarly aged children*, their abilities appear extraordinary. However, we are misled by this comparison, as it assumes their ability is part of who they are, the way they were born. Usually these children have been engaging in many more hours of practice than other children of their age.

We also incorrectly assume that the relative difference will continue, or become greater, later in life. In fact, extrapolating this way doesn't work, as most "gifted" children become relatively ordinary adults. In several famous studies of exceptionally gifted children, the majority went on to be barely distinguishable as adults.

As we've discussed, the only real measuring stick for talent is the ability to produce something valued by society – high-level adult performance. The child prodigy, while exceptional for their age, is not actually particularly good when compared on an adult scale. So, compared to adults who have been developing their abilities for 10 years or more, the typical prodigy is, in fact, not good at all.

Perhaps the most famous child prodigy was Mozart. The urban myth is that Mozart, born in 1756 in Austria, composed music when he was just six or seven years old. The problem with this myth is not its assertion that he composed as a child, because he did. The problem is how it fails to recognise the *quality* (compared to seasoned adults) of what he composed.

When we hear "Mozart composed", most people assume he was producing complex compositions, involving a full orchestra and playing for an hour or more. We assume his childhood compositions were like his adult compositions, of which we are familiar. The truth: he produced a 20-second piece for harpsichord. Impressive for a six-year-old, but hardly world class. Art historians tell us that Mozart didn't produce any work of enduring adult significance until he was about 21 years of age.

Section 3.2: The Rule of Practice

Before that, his works were notable for his age, but not significant when compared to other, more experienced composers.

But Mozart was exceptional, in that he was an exception. The world had never seen a 21-year-old composing and performing such significant works. At the time, composers didn't become world class until their early 30s, so Mozart was unique by comparison. He caused a sensation in the courts and wider musical world, because they had never seen his like before and *did not understand* how someone so young was so accomplished. To understand this aspect of his greatness, we need to dig further into his backstory.

Backstory: It Takes Time

Mozart's father, Leopold, was also a composer and performer. Importantly, he was an exceptional teacher of music. He was one of the few people in the world at the time who taught children music. In fact, he was so good at teaching children music, the book he wrote on the subject became a seminal work for the next 100 years.

Leopold forced Mozart to learn music from an early age. Research from the University of Exeter in the UK suggests that by the time Mozart wrote his 20-second piece for harpsichord, he had accumulated as many as 3000 hours of practice. Cast in this light, Mozart's short composition is important, but hardly exceptional. It could be argued that someone with 3000 hours of practice in music and composition should be able to compose short, original pieces.

At the time, most composers didn't start learning their craft until their mid-to-late teens. Young adults were taught music, but Mozart started when he was about five years of age. Most composers produced their first significant work in their early 30s, after about 15 years of learning their craft. Mozart produced his first significant work at 21 – *also after about 15 years of learning his craft.*

Mozart shares a similar backstory to other great composers. Far from being a natural who "saw a piano and could just play", he worked consistently, under the guidance of an expert, for about 15 years to develop his abilities. Mozart even makes this point himself. In a letter to his father, he wrote, "People make a great mistake who think my art has come easily to me. No one has devoted so much time and thought to composition as I".

We should absolutely celebrate exceptional achievers in all their different forms. As a composer, Mozart is among the best the world has ever experienced. But we should also be careful not to recognise Mozart, and others of exceptional ability, for "being" great, but for *what they did to become great*.

> Their most impressive achievement is not the performance, it is the years of hard work that went into developing the ability to perform.

What is the Cure for this Myth?

The cure for this myth is two-fold. First, we must ensure we use the right measuring stick when we celebrate and recognise achievements. We are right to celebrate Mozart's 20-second piece for harpsichord, but we should celebrate it for what it is: an impressive piece for a six-year-old. We should not perpetuate the myth that it is any more than that.

Secondly, we must always look to the backstory. As we will unpack in the following sections, the backstory to how abilities are acquired is critical if we are to close the Greatness Gap, develop a Growth Mindset and show students how they can grow and develop new, even exceptional, abilities.

Section 3.2: The Rule of Practice

Can All Prodigies Be Explained this Way?

Perhaps not. Perhaps there are a few unique individuals who, throughout history, have been born different. Without delving deeply into the backstory of each prodigy, it would be impossible to know for sure. Unfortunately, obtaining an accurate account of each backstory is difficult.

In his book, *Ungifted: Intelligence Redefined* (Basic Books, 2013), cognitive psychologist Scott Barry Kaufman describes the "perfect storm": a confluence of special factors that may be responsible for some individuals we call geniuses. Kaufman asserts that some people may be born with an innate predisposition to a particular ability. He says that if you are born with an advantage, if you are born into a family that recognises this advantage – a family that can nurture it by having access to facilities and teachers who can also help develop it – and if all this occurs within a society that values that ability, then truly exceptional performance may follow.

What I do know is that most people with exceptional abilities can be explained the same way. They have a backstory that contains similar elements of time, resources and the right sort of effort. Unpacking that backstory and demystifying the process by which talents and abilities are developed is important if we want students to understand that high-level achievement is not out of their reach, even if they are not (currently) a Mozart.

We create a powerful, negative Mindset Mover when we suggest that it's possible to acquire exceptional abilities without doing this work. Exceptional abilities aren't bestowed on a lucky few who were born that way. They are open to anyone who knows how to acquire them.

SECTION 3.3
The Rule of Effort

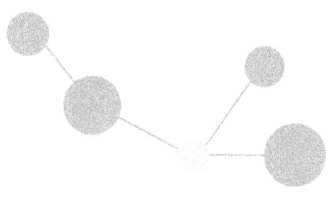

Effective Effort Leads to Growth

The Rule of Effort states that to increase your talents and abilities, you need to engage in Effective Effort. When we find a task difficult, we can apply Effective Effort to master that task and increase our abilities.

About Effort

Today, we have a deep understanding of how people at the top of their fields got there. The work of pioneers, such as Anders Ericsson, shows us that to achieve significant growth, we need to engage in many hours of Virtuous Practice. We recognise that each person we consider talented shares a common backstory that includes the slow development of that talent. In short, we recognise that everyone on the far side of the Greatness Gap took a journey to cross that gap.

However, while it is true to say that everyone who reaches the far side of the Greatness Gap follows a similar path, it is not true to say that everyone who sets out on that path gets across! There are many people with a Growth Mindset who engage in Virtuous Practice but do not achieve the growth they desire. For many people, the missing piece of the puzzle is effort. Not that they aren't willing to put in the effort – rather, they have been putting in the wrong sort of effort.

Usually when we talk about effort, we refer to the time and energy spent on a task. But Effective Effort involves more than simply time and energy. Effective Effort involves a set of behaviours, or Habits of Mind, that make the time and energy we spend *efficacious*.

But before we explore efficacy, we need to recognise the confused way in which we often talk about effort, and some of the negative Mindset Movers associated with it.

Negative Mindset Movers & the Rule of Effort

The word "effort" is used in many ways. Sometimes when we see someone progressing, we praise them for putting in a lot of effort and hard work. Other times, when someone isn't progressing, we praise them because "at least they are trying hard". For someone with a Growth Mindset, being praised for effort is rewarding and meaningful. But for someone with a Fixed Mindset, they can interpret it as having a deficit pointed out.

In this section, we will redefine effort by separating the sort of effort that leads to growth from other, less-productive forms of effort. But to do that, we must first be aware of how the way we use the word "effort" can create negative Mindset Movers.

When effort doesn't pay off

When we confuse effort with simply spending time and energy on a task, it can create the belief that effort does not always lead to growth, or that it is entirely reasonable to spend large amounts of time and energy practicing and not experience any growth.

It's also possible that someone with a Growth Mindset, who is prepared to step outside their Performance Zone and into their Learning Zone, may still experience little or no growth. They may engage in two of the 3 Fs – *focusing* on their goal and receiving *feedback* on their (lack of) progress – but be entirely unable to *fix it*!

As our time and energy mounts without progress, we come to "learn" that effort does not pay off. As a result, we may be inclined to stop putting in effort altogether. After all, if there has been no growth despite all that time and energy, why continue?

Effort makes up for a deficit

Effort is often portrayed as a desirable characteristic, but one only *necessary* for people without natural ability. The broad message is that *those who can* do so easily, while *those who can't* make up for it by having to work hard.

Consider this quote from high-school basketball coach Tim Notke: "Hard work beats talent when talent doesn't work hard." Embedded in that statement is the idea that hard work is a sign that you don't have natural talent; it's a sign of your deficit. This not only breaks the Rule of Practice, but also gives effort a bad name.

Even in our children's books, we see effort portrayed as making up for deficits in ability. Dweck (2006) discusses the story of *The Tortoise and the Hare*, and highlights how it shows the *need* for the tortoise to work hard because it is naturally slow. Most students, she points out, would probably want to be a slightly less foolish hare, who could easily cruise to victory with much less "effort" than the terminally slow tortoise.

It's little wonder that someone with a Fixed Mindset dislikes effort. They have bought into the messages above. For them, when someone praises their "effort", they feel that their deficits are being highlighted! "You must be a tortoise," they hear. "Keep up that hard work and hope that the hare doesn't wise up – you might have a chance at winning!" They believe that they *need* to put in effort because they are somehow lacking in "natural" ability.

Effort as the consolation prize

We hear it all the time from teachers and parents. Children are told, "It's okay, as long as you work hard." The message here is that as long as you're working hard, you can't be expected to achieve anything more, but you will reach *"your* best". Apparently, hard work will bring you to your natural limit, and for some students that natural limit is higher than others – one student's effort will take them further than another student's efforts.

This same message is often used as a consolation prize. As we've already discussed, our real rewards often go to students who have achieved the highest standard. Other students are given the consolation prize for their effort.

Effort's Been Getting a Bad Rap!

It's little wonder that for so many people, effort has a bad name. They've put in time and energy with the promise that it will result in growth, but they have failed to grow. They've seen others perform at a much higher level, doing more difficult things and doing them easily, when they have to work hard to achieve a lower standard of performance. And the world has told them that they can't expect anything more if they are working their hardest and not seeing progress.

Each of the above negative Mindset Movers contradict the Rule of Effort. If we want to develop more Growth-Oriented Mindsets in our students, we must first ensure that we send much clearer and positive messages about effort and, secondly, teach them how to engage in Effective Effort.

It's Not an Effort Mindset – It's a Growth Mindset

We must keep in mind that it is not an Effort Mindset we are trying to develop, it's a Growth Mindset. So it is not "okay, *as long as you work hard*".

> If the sort of effort you're engaging in is not leading to growth, then it's the wrong sort of effort!

At the end of the day, we are not as interested in effort as we are in efficacy. It is the outcome, the *effect* of the effort – the Growth – that matters. If our effort is not producing growth, then we need to understand why, and act to correct it so we can experience growth.

Of course, effort isn't always necessary. Some things are easy, so require little effort, whereas other things are hard, and therefore require more effort. The interesting question we need to answer, then, is: why do things that used to be hard, become easy? Or, how do we make hard things easy?

Habits of Mind

"Everything is hard before it is easy," said Johann Wolfgang von Goethe.

So, how do we make hard things easy? Why are some problems harder than others? More importantly, why are some people able to easily do the things that I find hard? And why today can I do easily some of the things I found difficult when I first encountered them? I seem to recall finding Year 4 particularly challenging, but I'm confident I could breeze through it today.

The issue is that "hard" is a relative term, not an absolute one. Problems are only hard until they become easy, and what is hard for one person may be easy for another. Problems and challenges aren't hard by nature – it is our (in)ability to know how to solve them that make them either hard or easy.

Apart from specific content knowledge about a problem, solving difficult problems requires us to behave in a certain way. It requires us to draw on a set of skills and dispositions that allow us to engage with and solve that problem. Persistence is one example. If we give up easily, the problem will remain unsolved. These behaviours, that allow us to solve difficult problems, define what it means to behave intelligently.

> To solve problems we find difficult, we need to behave intelligently. To solve increasingly difficult problems, we need to learn to behave increasingly intelligently.

Recall that Gardner defined intelligence as the ability to produce something that is valued by society. For Gardner, intelligence is defined by the ability to *do* something, and eventually produce something – a work of art, a solution to a mathematical problem, a successful business, etc. – that society values.

Society tends to value most highly the things not everyone can do, or the things most people find difficult. To do these things, you need to behave very intelligently – in fact, more intelligently than anyone else. The people who can do the most difficult things produce the things most valued by society. Therefore, they are by definition the most intelligent people in our society.

Section 3.3: The Rule of Effort

Note that we are not talking about intelligence as a fixed trait – something you were born with. We are talking about intelligence as the behaviours we've learnt that allow us to produce something valued by society. To draw on the racing-car analogy from earlier in this section, we are talking about the driving skills you've acquired, and not the car you were born with.

Consider again the Learning Plateau we discussed earlier. Notice that the vertical axis denotes the level of difficulty. As we attempt increasingly difficult tasks, we initially succeed because we are smart enough to do those tasks. They are "easy things we haven't done yet".

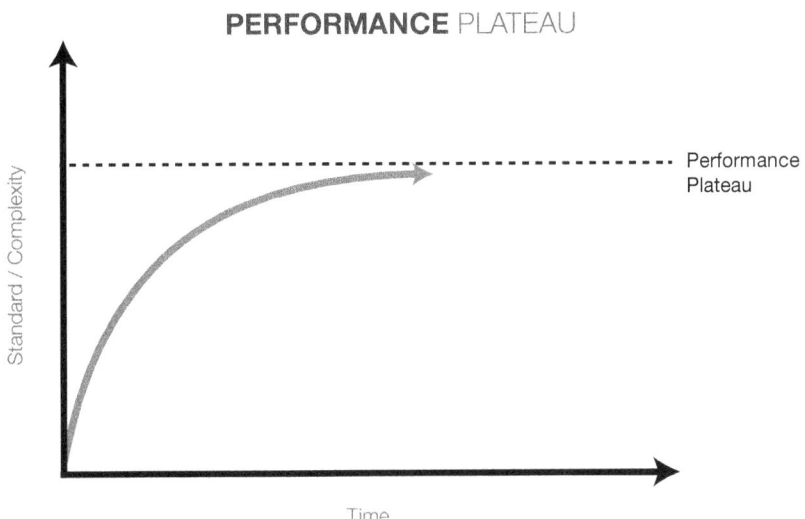

But at some stage, we reach a point where the tasks become difficult and we may stop seeing progress: a Performance Plateau. You could think of this plateau as the limit of our (current) intelligence. We literally aren't smart enough (yet) to work beyond that level of difficulty, so we need to get smarter! We need to develop the sorts of behaviours that will allow us to solve more difficult behaviours. We need to learn how to behave more intelligently.

What Does It Look Like to Behave Intelligently?

If the ability to solve difficult problems requires us to learn, master and draw on a particular set of behaviours, the critical question arises: what are those behaviours? This is exactly the question Art Costa and Bena Kallick have answered for us.

Where Anders Ericsson essentially examined a person's backstory, paying close attention to the process they undertook to develop their abilities, Art Costa and Bena Kallick (2008) described the *behaviours* required to engage in that process successfully. As peak performers engaged in Virtuous Practice, attempting and mastering increasingly difficult tasks, Costa described the behaviours they adopted. Initially, Costa described these as Intelligent Behaviours, which later came to be known as "Habits of Mind".

Habits of Mind

When Art Costa first described what would become known as the Habits of Mind, he used the term "intelligent behaviours".

"Intelligent behaviours," he said, "are demonstrated when we are confronted with questions and problems *for which we don't know an immediate answer*" (Costa, 1985). In other words, he described the behaviours demonstrated when people were challenged with difficult tasks.

Costa had identified these behaviours based on other researchers' descriptions of what the most intelligent people do. These were people at the top of their field, who worked on the most difficult problems and achieved the highest standards, and so, by Gardner's definition, would be considered among the most intelligent people in the community. Costa recognised and described these people as engaging in a set of behaviours he called the 16 Habits of Mind.

Section 3.3: The Rule of Effort

HABITS OF MIND

1. Persisting

Stick to it! Persevering in task through to completion; remaining focused. Looking for ways to reach your goal when stuck. Not giving up.

2. Managing impulsivity

Take your Time! Thinking before acting; remaining calm, thoughtful and deliberative.

3. Listening with understanding and empathy

Understand Others! Devoting mental energy to another person's thoughts and ideas. Make an effort to perceive another's point of view and emotions.

4. Thinking flexibly

Look at it Another Way! Being able to change perspectives, generate alternatives, consider options.

5. Thinking about your thinking (Metacognition)

Know your knowing! Being aware of your own thoughts, strategies, feelings and actions and their effects on others.

6. Striving for accuracy

Check it again! Always doing your best. Setting high standards. Checking and finding ways to improve constantly.

7. Questioning and problem posing

How do you know? Having a questioning attitude; knowing what data are needed and developing questioning strategies to produce those data. Finding problems to solve.

8. Applying past knowledge to new situations

Use what you Learn! Accessing prior knowledge; transferring knowledge beyond the situation in which it was learned.

9. Thinking and communicating with clarity and precision

Be clear! Striving for accurate communication in both written and oral form; avoiding over generalizations, distortions, deletions and exaggerations.

10. Gather data through all senses

Use your natural pathways! Pay attention to the world around you Gather data through all the senses; taste, touch, smell, hearing and sight.

11. Creating, imagining, and innovating

Try a different way! Generating new and novel ideas, fluency, originality

12. Responding with wonderment and awe

Have fun figuring it out! Finding the world awesome, mysterious and being intrigued with phenomena and beauty.

13. Taking responsible risks

Venture out! Being adventuresome; living on the edge of one's competence. Try new things constantly.

14. Finding Humor

Laugh a little! Finding the whimsical, incongruous and unexpected. Being able to laugh at oneself.

15. Thinking interdependently

Work together! Being able to work in and learn from others in reciprocal situations. Team work.

16. Remaining open to continuous learning

I have so much more to learn! Having humility and pride when admitting we don't know; resisting complacency.

www.jamesanderson.com.au
Source: *Habits of Mind Across the Curriculum: Practical and Creative Strategies for Teachers.*
By Arthur L. Costa and Bena Kallick. Alexandria, VA. ASCD. © 2009. Reproduced with Permission. Visit www.ascd.org

Download this infographic in full size from
www.jamesanderson.com.au/p/TheAgileLearnerDownloads/

But as useful and powerful as this picture was, it was incomplete.

These people weren't simply "demonstrating" Habits of Mind, they were exhibiting how to use them in their most skilful, mature and highly developed form.

Recognising the importance of development, Costa and Kallick (2008) came to define the Habits of Mind as: "The dispositions that are *skilfully* and *mindfully* employed by characteristically successful people when confronted with problems, the solutions to which are not immediately apparent."

It's not that the people who have reached the highest level of performance "use" the Habits of Mind and other people don't, it's that these people have learnt how to use them more effectively and skilfully than other people. This means they can solve the most difficult problems and progress further than anyone else, because they have learnt how to behave more intelligently.

In this light, it became clear that the teachers' role in schools was not to teach the Habits of Mind, but to help students continually develop them and learn how to behave increasingly intelligently, so that they become capable of solving increasingly difficult tasks.

Learning to Behave More Intelligently

Understanding that intelligence is not an inherited fixed trait, but one to be developed over time, leads us to focus not only on the "use" of the Habits of Mind, but on their development. We learn to become better at *Persisting*. We improve our capacity to *Manage Impulsivity*. We enhance our skills in *Creating, Imagining* and *Innovating*. We become

Section 3.3: The Rule of Effort

more mature in our ability to *Apply Past Knowledge to New Situations*. We heighten our ability to *Listen with Understanding and Empathy*. We become more skilful at *Questioning and Posing Problems*.

One of the challenges for schools working with Habits of Mind is knowing what it looks like to get better at them. We can say we want students to get better at Persisting, but what exactly does that entail? We can recognise that one person is better at Managing Impulsivity than another, but precisely how do you describe that difference? What do you have to learn to be better?

What Art Costa had initially described was the end point of a long backstory of development of intelligent behaviours. While these people were displaying well-developed Habits of Mind, it wasn't clear how that development had been facilitated, and how someone else might follow a similar path and learn to behave more intelligently.

In fact, because the backstory of the Habits of Mind hadn't been adequately articulated, some teachers saw the Habits of Mind as confirmation of the Greatness Gap. People with (well-developed) Habits of Mind were intelligent and could do difficult things, and the reason why some students couldn't do difficult things was because they didn't "have" the (well-developed) Habits of Mind. For these teachers, the Habits of Mind became a de facto way of identifying fixed intelligence. Of course, this was never Costa and Kallick's intention, so we needed a way to describe what the development of the Habits of Mind looked like.

To address this, I teamed with Costa and Kallick and, in 2006, we published the Dimensions of Growth for the Habits of Mind, which represent the ways in which learners can grow within each Habit of Mind. While they don't represent a complete description of development, they do describe the pathways along which growth can take place.

Briefly, these dimensions are

- Meaning: We seek a deeper, more insightful, more sophisticated understanding of the Habit
- Capacity: We build an increasing repertoire of skills, strategies and techniques through which we engage in the Habit
- Alertness: We become more finely attuned to the signals and cues in a situation that tell us when we should and shouldn't engage in one or more of the Habits of Mind
- Value: We come to better recognise the benefits and advantages of engaging in the Habits of Mind. We place increasingly high value on them and choose to engage in them over less-productive behaviours
- Commitment: We become more committed to the ongoing development of the Habits of Mind. We learn to be increasingly self-assessing, self-directed and self-monitoring in our development of the Habits.

Taken together, these dimensions of growth describe what it looks like to develop the Habits of Mind and learn to behave more intelligently.

Section 3.3: The Rule of Effort

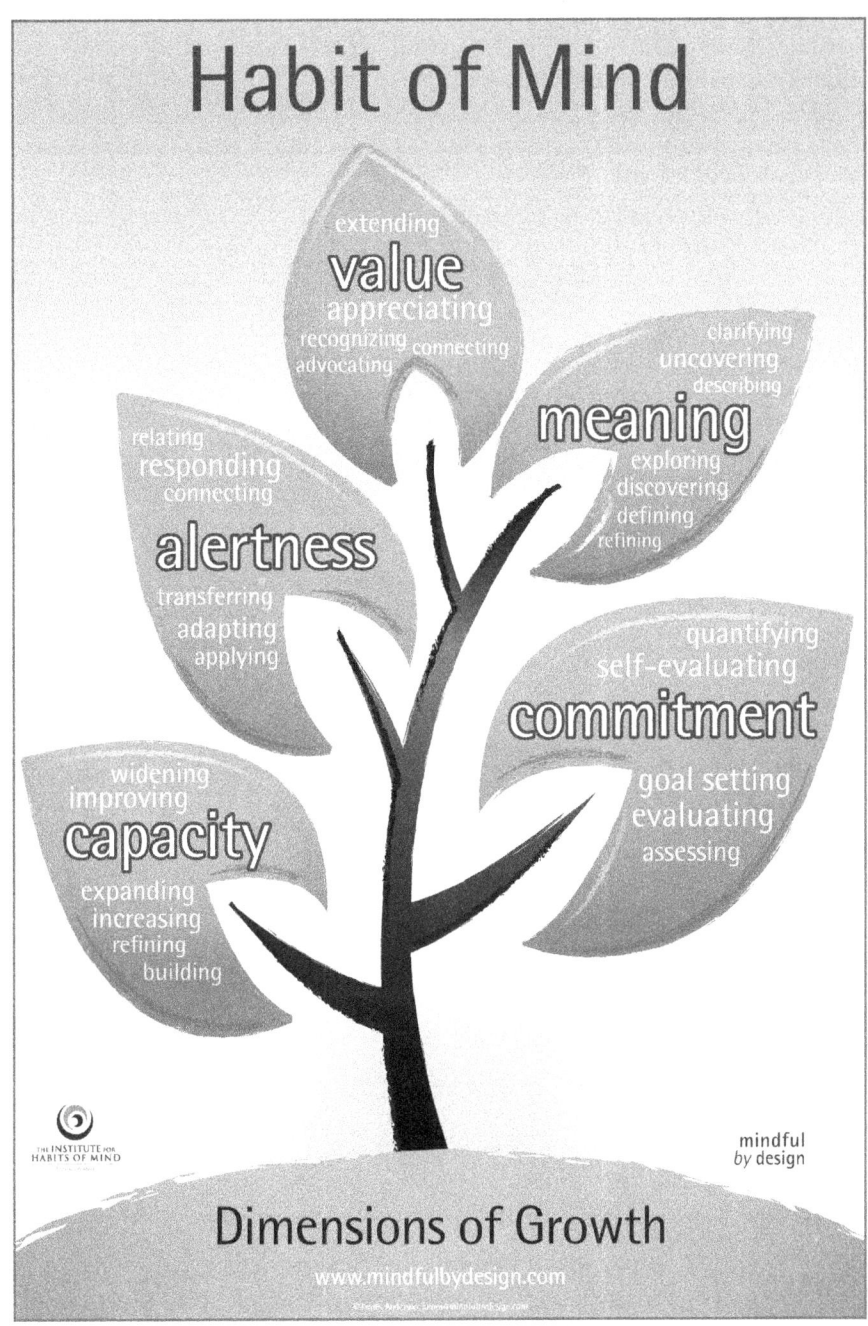

Download this infographic in full size from
www.jamesanderson.com.au/p/TheAgileLearnerDownloads/

Learning Power

As we develop our Habits of Mind, our capacity for doing difficult things increases. We learn to behave more intelligently, and in doing so we develop a critical component of both Learning Agility and the Rule of Effort: Learning Power.

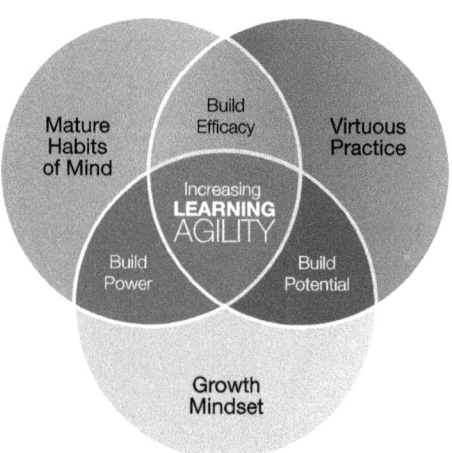

Our Learning Power is a measure of the development of our Habits of Mind, or the behaviours that allow us to do increasingly difficult tasks. It is a result of applying our Growth Mindset to our Habits of Mind. Learning Power allows us to engage increasingly successfully with increasingly challenging tasks.

There are two critical outcomes of the development of Learning Power:

We increase our "easy things we haven't done yet"

If you've ever met someone with lots of Learning Power, they were probably quite good at something. They have likely combined and applied their Learning Power and specific content knowledge to master difficult things in a certain area. They may have even been considered an expert or successful in their chosen field.

Section 3.3: The Rule of Effort

People who are great at one thing are often pretty good at lots of things, as they find that they can "turn their hand" to many tasks. This is not an argument for generalisable intelligence, but rather is an acknowledgement that many of the behaviours that help you master one area are reasonably transferable.

Being an expert in one domain does not make you an expert in other domains – you must develop specific content-area expertise – but many of the behaviours that made you an expert in your chosen field can be applied to new domains.

For example, aspects of your ability to work interdependently in your sport domain can be transferred to your business domain. Furthermore, a counsellor's well-developed skills of Listening with Understanding and Empathy may also be applied productively to their parenting. These 21st-century skills – the Habits of Mind – are highly sought after by employers for the very reason that they can be, at least in part, transferable to new situations, making the person with Learning Power highly versatile.

Consider again the Performance Plateau diagrams below. As your Learning Power increases, you're able to do increasingly difficult things – you effectively "raise the bar". Your Learning Zone is always the standard slightly above your current standard, and your Performance Zone is always your highest standard.

"Raising the Bar" like this increases the number of things that would fall into your Comfort Zone of "easy things you haven't done yet". Because of this, Learning Power increases your versatility. It's a critical component of Learning Agility because it equips you with a set of skills that can be applied in new contexts.

PERFORMANCE PLATEAU 1

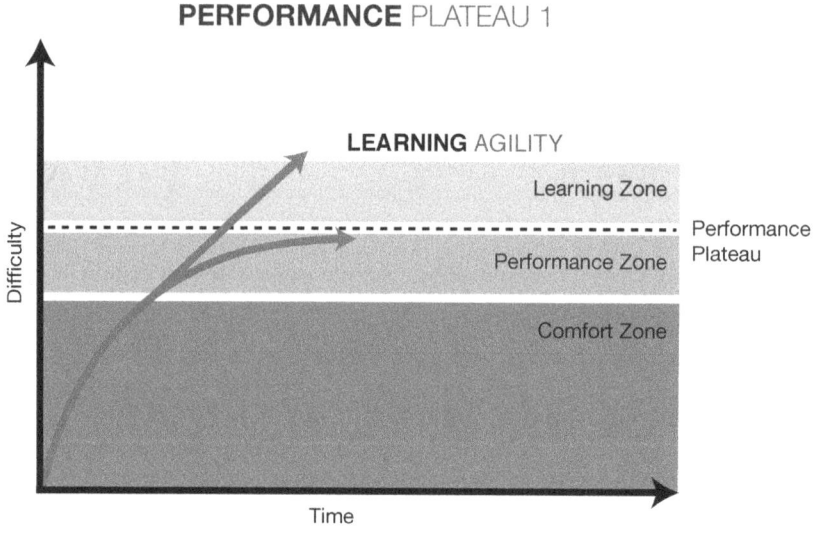

Increasing your learning power "raises the bar" of our peak performance. While our Performance and Learning Zones remain the same size, our Comfort Zone increases. This effectively increases the number of things that are "easy things we haven't done yet".

PERFORMANCE PLATEAU 2

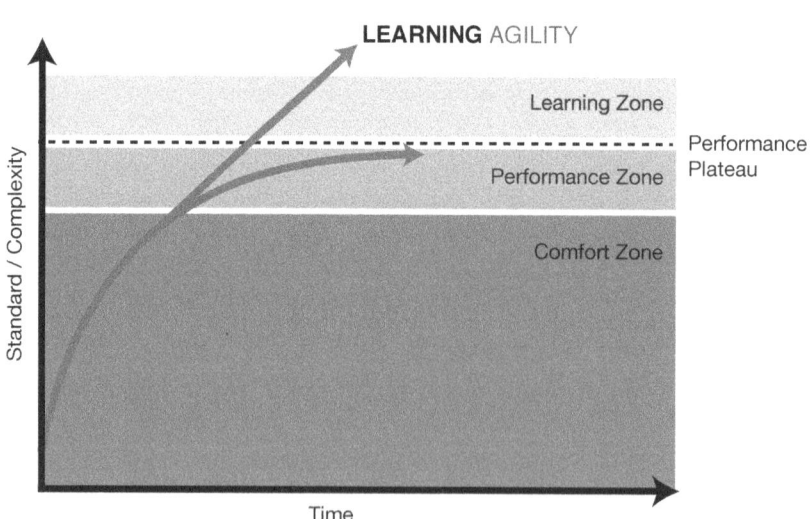

Section 3.3: The Rule of Effort

Effective Effort

As we noted earlier, everything is hard until it becomes easy. We make hard things easy by developing Learning Power.

As we develop Learning Power, we learn to behave more intelligently. This means tasks that were once difficult become easier. When combined with specific content knowledge, it gives us the capacity to solve problems we couldn't previously solve.

When we combine our understanding of what it means to develop our Habits of Mind with our understanding of Virtuous Practice, it gives us a pathway for *efficacy*. We begin to understand why not all sorts of effort are equal, and why the negative Mindset Movers discussed at the start of this section were wrong in one critical aspect: they referred to the wrong sorts of effort. In the next section, we will explore what we mean by Effective Effort.

Effective Effort

Not all types of effort are equal. When we combine our understanding of the development of Costa and Kallick's Habits of Mind with our understanding of Ericsson's work on practice, we can describe four different types of effort, only one of which results in growth.

The Effective Effort Matrix

Effort is more than spending time and energy on a task. It is about the type of practice we engage in (where we are practicing) and the types of behaviours we bring to that practice (how we are practicing).

EFFECTIVE EFFORT MATRIX

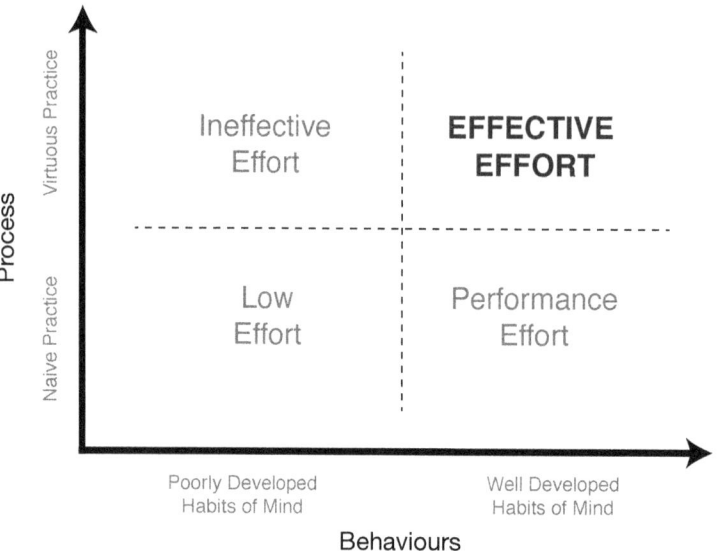

Looking at the vertical axis of the Effective Effort Matrix, we see that it is divided into Naive Practice and Virtuous Practice. As described earlier, this relates to whether we are practicing in our Learning Zone. The horizontal axis relates to the development of our Habits of Mind. It asks if we are engaging in our most highly developed Habits of Mind, and therefore behaving most intelligently, or if we are engaging with our Habits of Mind at a low level.

The resulting matrix defines for us four types of effort. Each type of effort has a different outcome, and only one, Effective Effort, leads to growth.

Learning to recognise that what we've traditionally called "effort" does not always lead to growth helps us to better identify the type of effort we need to help students engage in. It helps teachers to both direct students toward more efficacious effort and understand why effort has been getting such a bad reputation.

Types of Effort

Low Effort: Taking the easy road

When students work on tasks that are too easy for them, they are engaging in Low Effort. There is no real intellectual stretch and the task requires only basic skills. These sorts of tasks may have been mastered long ago and can be "done with your eyes closed".

Because the work is easy, the quality is likely to be high with few errors. The student might be expending time and energy, but they aren't learning anything new. Answering the easiest questions where the answer is already known or easily produced is an example of Low Effort.

Low Effort is also seen when doing "easy things you haven't done yet". You already have the pre-requisite behaviours, so you're not being stretched. At best, this sort of effort results in being able to do more things, but not more difficult things.

Performance Effort: Doing your best

Students engaged in Performance Effort produce their best, most reliable work. They are in their Performance Zone, usually using their most well-developed Habits of Mind to reach their highest standard.

When engaged in Performance Effort, students try to minimise mistakes and so learning opportunities are reduced. Ironically, this low error rate can often make it appear as though the student is "doing it easy".

Outwardly, there might be little difference between someone engaged in Low Effort and someone engaged in Performance Effort. Both have a low error rate and, unless you know something about the person's standard, it can be hard to tell how close to their limit they are.

There are certainly times when we want students to engage in Performance Effort. Remember that when you go beyond your Performance Zone, your standard decreases. So anytime we want students to demonstrate their best work, their highest standard, they need to engage in Performance Effort. However this does not lead to further improvement.

Engaging in Performance Effort may result in a more reliable performance, as you repeat and rehearse your current best work, but it does not produce an increase in ability. You may become more reliable, but you won't become better.

Low Effort and Performance Effort contribute to negative Mindset Movers by making performance look easy. Remember, "hard" is a relative term, and one person's Low Effort might be challenging for another person at that point in time.

Imagine trying to learn a new piece on the piano. You've been learning for 12 months, and this is the hardest piece you've tried yet. You're making lots of mistakes and struggling. Someone who has been playing for 10 years sits next to you. It's a piece they've never seen before either, but they pick it up easily. For the advanced student, it's an "easy thing they haven't done yet", because they have the prerequisite skills to master it, making it look easy.

Whenever we see someone else perform with low errors, and when we are unaware of their backstory of errors and effort that led to that level of performance, it can make it appear that our effort is required to make up for a deficit.

It's not entirely surprising that Low Effort and Performance Effort don't result in significant growth, as they both break the Rule of Practice because they are not in the Learning Zone. However the big challenge we face when we talk about effort is Ineffective Effort.

Section 3.3: The Rule of Effort

Ineffective Effort: Working hard, getting nowhere

When we stretch ourselves, and attempt a standard that's higher than our best, we expect to fail. After all, if we could perform at that level, it would be our best. However, for many people, their first failure leads to their second, and then their third. They find that what they can't do "yet" becomes what they still can't do yet!

The trouble with Ineffective Effort is that it occurs in our Learning Zone. It holds to the Rule of Practice, but the behaviours that would allow us to learn and master that level of performance are absent. The Habits of Mind we are applying to the task are not up to the job! The student is attempting a task they're not intelligent enough to master!

When we engage in Ineffective Effort, energy and time are high, as are errors and, often, concentration. We may see what needs to be achieved, but are unable to see how to achieve it. Results are low and improvements are minimal, or non-existent.

It is this sort of effort that gives "effort" a bad name. Students try something difficult and spend time and energy on the task, but see no result. If too much time is spent engaged in this sort of effort, students' performance will plateau and they will go through the cascade of emotions that we explored in the opening section of this book. Eventually students will come to learn that effort doesn't pay off, and will stop putting in any time and energy.

Unfortunately, this sort of effort is often praised as a consolation prize. The student is "trying", but not being effective. In the Fixed Mindset world, they have reached their limit, and the best we can do is encourage them to continue to work harder in the hope that enough hard work will eventually make up for the deficit. We encourage the tortoise to run for longer to try to catch up to the hare.

> The trouble is that more time and energy isn't the answer. The answer is learning to spend that time and energy more *intelligently*.

The student is going nowhere because they haven't yet learnt to behave intelligently enough. To progress, they need to be taught how to behave more intelligently and, ironically, when they have learnt to behave more intelligently, the time and energy they expend decreases!

Effective Effort: Growth and learning

To grow and master more difficult things, we need to get into our Learning Zone and attempt more difficult tasks, but we also must learn to behave more intelligently. We need to focus on *how* we are learning – our behaviours and Habits of Mind – not just *what* we are trying to learn.

Moving from Naive Practice to Virtuous Practice is relatively easy. We need only challenge ourselves or have a difficult task forced on us. The point is that this movement happens in a moment. We simply confront the challenging task.

To learn to behave more intelligently takes time, and requires its own 3 Fs. We need to know what the more intelligent behaviour looks like, so we'll need to understand and *focus* on the Dimensions of Growth for the Habits of Mind. We'll need to get *feedback* about how close we are to mastering our new behaviours, and we'll need guidance to ensure we can *fix it* and master different ways of working.

We still make mistakes when we engage in Effective Effort, but they are stretch mistakes – the kind that guide our learning. As we respond effectively to those mistakes, our abilities increase and mistakes decrease.

The result of responding effectively to stretch mistakes is that you "raise the bar" of your performance. Not only do you master the specific task you're working on, but because you've become more intelligent, you are capable of more "easy things you haven't done yet".

How and When to Praise Effort

There is a lot of talk about praising effort. The intent of this has always been to encourage students to work hard so they can achieve growth. However, in practice we are quite possibly undermining students' growth – unless we get much better at the way we praise effort.

The challenge teachers have with praising effort is twofold:

Effective Effort versus other forms of effort

When we praise students for Low Effort, Performance Effort or Ineffective Effort, we encourage them to engage in behaviours that don't lead to growth. Further, if our overarching message is that "effort" is required for growth and we encourage students to engage in Low Effort, Performance Effort or Ineffective Effort, then they will learn that their efforts don't lead to growth. The Rule of Effort will appear to be broken.

The False Mindset

As we discussed in Section 2, someone has a False Mindset when they intellectually understand the importance of a Growth Mindset, yet they have not spent time reflecting deeply on their own Mindset. This person might have Mindset Moments, such as consciously choosing to engage positive Mindset Movers such as praising student effort, but many of their day-to-day decisions may be guided by the unconscious bias of their more Fixed Mindset.

As a result, their well-intended "praise effort" may become "praise the struggling students for effort". When we inadvertently send the message that more effort is required for some students than others, we unintentionally create the Greatness Gap and reinforce the negative Mindset Mover that effort makes up for a deficit.

How to Praise Effort – Effectively!

As educators, we should recognise, reward and praise students' effort, but we must do it in a way that recognises the essential role of Effective Effort in achieving growth.

Effective Effort is a common element of the backstory to every achievement. Teaching students how to engage in it, and recognise its importance, is a critical learning outcome at all levels.

> At the end of the day, it is the effect of the effort, the growth, that we are trying to achieve.

To praise effort effectively, we first must learn to distinguish between Effective Effort and the sorts of effort that don't lead to growth (Low, Performance and Ineffective). It is not that these other forms of effort are bad, it is simply that they are incomplete. Each time we see students engaged in effort that isn't leading to growth, we need to recognise the specific behaviours and actions required for growth, then direct them towards Effective Effort.

For example, when we see students engaged in Low Effort, we should recognise that being on task, focusing, concentrating and engaging in some of the Habits of Mind (even at a low level) is a good thing. We then must point out that we don't learn by doing easy things, we learn

Section 3.3: The Rule of Effort

by doing hard things – things that challenge and stretch us. Having recognised the aspects of Low Effort we want to see continue, we direct students towards more efficacious behaviours.

For the student engaged in Performance Effort, there is much to be recognised and rewarded. It's good to see a student doing their best. They are behaving intelligently and engaging in their most well-developed Habits of Mind. To achieve this level, the student must have previously struggled with Effective Effort. We should recognise that there has been a successful backstory for the student to have reached this point. This student is demonstrating their mastery, their peak performance, and they are likely proud that there are few, if any, mistakes.

While mastery is great, our real goal in the classroom is learning. We need to point out to this student that to continue to grow, they must step out of their Performance Zone and into their Learning Zone again by trying something more difficult. This might result in mistakes, but we assure them that we expect mistakes when learning new things.

For students engaging in Ineffective Effort, again there is much we want to recognise and praise. We want to praise that they are working on something hard enough for them to learn from. We also want to recognise that they have tried several ways to reach a solution, which is great, but that those strategies haven't worked. We then want them to recognise that to progress and master this level of difficulty, the student must learn more strategies to improve and develop their Habits of Mind, so that they can learn to behave more intelligently.

Note that in the examples above we do not praise students for their "effort". We praise and recognise the specific aspects of their behaviours that are likely to lead to growth, and then direct them towards more effective effort.

The word "effort" has a pervasive influence in our schools and broader society. Unfortunately, it is often confused with time and energy spent on a task, and not always with growth. I doubt that it would be possible for teachers to start using the language of the Effective Effort Matrix in classrooms. We are unlikely to hear, "Great Effective Effort today!"

As educators, we can be more explicit, more intentional and more focused in the way we praise effort. If we only use the word "effort" when we see Effective Effort, praise the specific behaviours that are likely to lead to growth, and direct students towards more productive, efficacious behaviours. That is when students will come to better understand "effort" as a process that leads to growth, rather than simply time and energy spent on a task.

The Rule of Effective Effort

When all is said and done, it is Effective Effort that leads to growth. This potent combination of Virtuous Practice and powerful Habits of Mind is at the heart of achieving growth in any area.

Effective Effort is even more important than a Growth Mindset. You can achieve growth, even significant growth, without a Growth Mindset simply by engaging in Effective Effort. The number of people Carol Dweck (2006) describes in her book and research who have a Fixed Mindset is a testament to the fact that you don't need a Growth Mindset to grow – you simply need to behave in the right way.

A Growth Mindset is important because it means you are more likely to engage in the behaviours that lead to growth – it is an invitation to grow. It helps you understand that when you encounter difficulties, you've not reached some sort of limit. You understand that you have the capacity to respond to these difficulties successfully and grow.

Section 3.3: The Rule of Effort

The Rule of Effort holds that to grow, you must engage in Effective Effort.

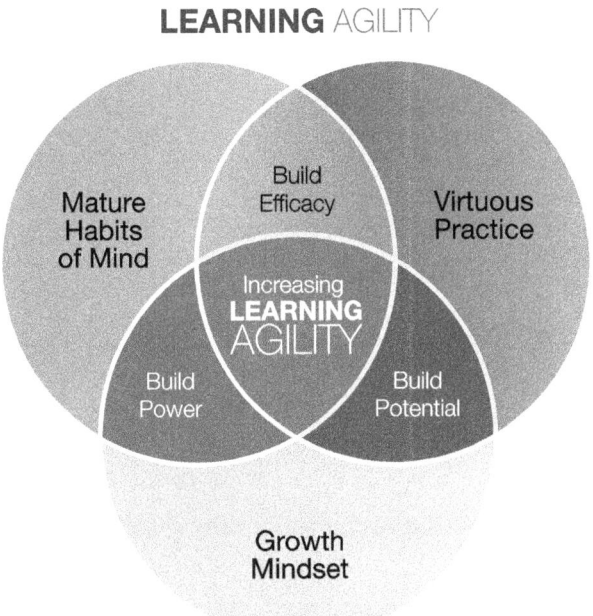

SECTION 3.4
The Rule of Unlimited Growth

About Potential

The Rule of Unlimited Growth speaks to your potential. It flies in the face of much of what we have traditionally been told about a person's capacity to achieve.

When you search for the word "potential" online, you'll find it is often accompanied by words such as "reaching", "achieving", "fulfilling" and "unlocking". In the wider community, potential is often thought of as a limited commodity. It's built into who you are: how much of it you have depends on what you were born with, and it dictates how much you can achieve. US President Theodore Roosevelt captured this idea when he said, "You can't choose your potential, but you can choose to fulfil it."

The idea that some people have more potential for growth than others is so pervasive that we barely notice its influence on us. We talk about one person's potential glowingly, and another person's gravely. We say that some people have "so much potential", and lament others for "wasting" theirs.

Take a moment to reflect on your own unconscious views of potential. Consider two students in your classroom: one whom you regard as having high potential and another whom you regard as having less potential. Imagine that you meet them again when they are in their early 30s. By any measure you want to use, they are doing the same things. Are you excited and pleased for how well the "low-potential student" has done? Are you disappointed that the "high-potential student" hasn't done better?

Of course, not everyone sees potential this way. Sometimes we talk about not knowing what you can achieve – that you can't know a person's potential. But I usually find most people with the "unknowable" view of potential also "know" that some people have more of it than others!

When we encourage people to reach *"their"* potential, inferring that theirs is different to someone else's, we tell them that the Greatness Gap is real. We talk about learning as a way of reaching "your" potential, which is different to someone else's potential. When we say things like "not everyone can be good at that", we say that the amount of growth one person is capable of achieving is different to another person.

The way we traditionally talk about a person's potential can be a powerful negative Mindset Mover. There is a subtlety to it that tries to subvert the other Four Rules About Talent. Talking about potential recognises that you must practice and apply effort. Your potential is unrealised until you engage in the Rules of Practice and Effort.

On the one hand, it acknowledges that we must work hard, but on the other, it gives us an "out" when we don't achieve. We couldn't have expected to achieve too much because we didn't have the potential for it!

We also break the Rule of Choice by saying that someone has more or less potential in a particular field. We tell children that while they might be good at a number of things, their "true" potential only lies in one area.

Each time we fall back on a person's limited potential as an excuse for them to cease growing, we create a negative Mindset Mover and break the Rule of Unlimited Growth. This rule not only tells us that there is no Greatness Gap, it also tells us there's no end to growth – you can always keep improving. It's not that you are ever "talented" – it's that you can continue to become *increasingly talented*.

Is there ever a point at which a person cannot become more talented? Do they reach a stage where it's impossible for them to continue to improve? Perhaps, but I doubt it. We'll never truly know if anyone's potential is completely unlimited, but we have good reason to believe that if there is a limit, we haven't come close to it yet. The evidence lies in history, and in your brain.

How Do We Know Your Potential Growth Is Unlimited?

Some of the best evidence for the Rule of Unlimited Potential lies in the history of human performance. History is full of bests that were bettered as each generation outperformed the last. Each generation has pushed the boundaries of human performance to a new level, so that previous "bests" have become commonplace.

This is a vindication for the Rule of Practice. Recall that there are two types of Virtuous Practice: Deliberate and Purposeful. Deliberate Practice involves a proven path to expertise, with guidance from someone who has walked that path before. Because the pathway is well understood, the mistakes are known and the strategies to avoid or correct them have been mastered. Progress can be relatively quick.

It is at the edge of known human performance that progress is slower. Purposeful Practice is employed when the way forward is not so well defined. The person at the peak of human performance is a trail blazer: they must mark out the territory, make the mistakes and work out the path forward. This is time-consuming, and often involves the need to develop new thinking and techniques. But once the path is known, others can follow their footsteps more quickly and attain the same level of performance in less time.

Ericsson makes this point throughout his book, *Peak*. He points to achievements in sport, such as the marathon, middle-distance running and high board diving, where performances once thought impossible are now commonplace. In intellectual fields such as chess playing, the games and faults of past grandmasters are analysed by players considered merely good by today's standards. In classical music, techniques once thought extraordinary are now routinely performed by thousands. Clearly, our human "best" is getting better.

If human potential was truly limited, recognising that today's standards are much higher than those of the past, we'd have to assume that previous generations weren't doing their best. Further, because I'm convinced that all people at the peak of human performance today are doing their best – they aren't holding back – we'd have to assume that we are living in a time where we've reached "peak performance" – and little, if any, further improvement is possible!

An alternative explanation for why today's performances surpass past performances is that we are somehow enriching human potential in each new generation. Perhaps only the people with the highest potential are breeding, thus their potential is being concentrated in future generations?

Both these explanations – that we've reached peak performance and we're enriching human potential – are clearly implausible. So, we are left with the undeniable truth that human potential is growing and there is no limit – at least not one we've encountered. The history of human potential is one of unlimited growth.

However, the fact that *human* potential holds to the Rule of Unlimited Growth does not necessarily mean every *individual's* potential is unlimited. It might be that the opportunity to develop potential in our communities is increasing. Perhaps previous generations did have an enormous untapped reservoir of human potential, and the difference today is that we can identify and develop that potential. Perhaps we are simply finding more individuals with potential now than we ever did in the past. Perhaps our education systems and the ability to specialise have both been so greatly enhanced that we're able to allow more people to develop and get closer to their potential.

While the above is possible, there is good evidence to show why everyone's potential should be unlimited. It explains why, although we all have the sense that we are doing our best today, our best can become better. And it makes clear why things that were once hard become easier. The evidence lies in our brain and its ability to change.

Brain Plasticity

We used to think of the brain as a static machine. Hardwired at or just after birth, its predetermined structure accounted for why some people had abilities others did not. Sure, we needed to learn, but because we saw the brain as fixed we considered learning as a way of reaching our potential and tapping into what was already there.

There was good reason for thinking this way. When people injured their brains, they often didn't get much better. Paralysis was permanent. Brain injuries due to stroke, cancer or physical injury often caused permanent disabilities. Unlike most other parts of the body that were capable of at least some level of repair, "broken brains" usually did not heal at all.

In recent times, we've started to understand that the brain is capable of healing itself. Ground-breaking research, skilfully outlined in books such as Norman Doidge's *The Brain That Changes Itself* (Viking Press, 2007) and *The Brain's Way of Healing* (Penguin Books Limited, 2015), illustrates the brain's remarkable capability to rewire itself, even in the face of significant damage. Moreover, the brain's ability to change and adapt has been shown to go well beyond simply repairing damaged structures. When a broken leg heals, a new bone similar to the old one is created. When the brain heals, the damaged area often remains, but new connections are formed within the brain to replace the previous function using entirely new neural pathways. This ability to rewire goes even further, as it's not simply a case of repairing or rebuilding to replace function. The brain can rewire itself in ways that lead to the development of new functions!

Remarkable research has shown how the brain responds to learning. In the brains of people learning to read braille, the area responsible for detecting touch increases in size, giving them greater sensitivity, and therefore improving their ability to read braille. No such changes occur in blind people who do not learn to read braille. In a similar way, the brain's representation of a guitar player's left hand, which is responsible for the complex fingering involved in playing different chords, is larger and more complex than the representation of the player's right hand, which only strums the guitar.

Furthermore, the brain's capacity to rewire and develop new abilities is not limited to physical abilities. In one study of London taxi drivers (Maguire, Woollett & Spiers, 2006), researchers looked at what changes took place in the brain as the drivers developed their ability to navigate London's streets. Over the course of a year, researchers saw an increase in the drivers' ability to navigate London's streets and in their ability to solve spatial awareness problems. These improvements occurred alongside structural changes in their brains. Over the same period, bus drivers who followed the same route every day and did not need to learn to navigate a new route experienced no changes in their brain structures.

Indeed, there is a growing body of compelling evidence that shows the brain is far from being the static, fragile machine we once thought it to be. We now understand that the brain constantly rewires itself, changing the connections between neurons, the strength of these connections and the speed at which electrical impulses are conducted and transmitted. In short, the brain is not hardwired – it is incredibly plastic.

Section 3.4: The Rule of Unlimited Growth

The idea of brain plasticity dramatically changes our old views of potential, while also shedding light on the Four Rules About Talent.

Considering what we know about brain plasticity, we now recognise that the reason you can't do the "hard things you haven't done yet" is because your brain is literally not wired for it. This means you are working to the absolute limit of your (current) potential. It's not that you have abilities locked away, waiting to be accessed. Instead you must build these new abilities by developing new neural pathways that will allow you to do things you couldn't before.

As Anders Ericsson puts it, learning is not a way of reaching your potential, it is a way of developing it. That development is done through the creation of new connections in your brain.

> Seen in this light, the role of the teacher is akin to the role of neural engineer. The result of the teaching process is a rewiring of students' brains so they are capable of doing things they could not do before.

It's interesting to note that when Carol Dweck first set out to help students develop a more Growth-Oriented Mindset, she did not teach students about Mindsets. She did not tell them, "A Growth Mindset is good, you should have one of these!" Instead, she taught students about the brain's capacity to change as a result of learning. Her flagship strategy for developing a Growth Mindset, "Brainology", teaches students about their "amazing plastic brain".

Four Rules About Talent – In Light of Brain Plasticity

Early in this book, I pointed out that a Growth Mindset would not work if the underlying reality was that each individual was not actually capable of growth. Simply believing you could grow wasn't enough – you had to know how to grow. As we have examined the Four Rules About Talent, we've looked at what you must do to achieve that growth. Brain plasticity is the underlying reality of the Four Rules About Talent.

The reason the Rule of Choice holds is that no-one has a well-developed brain in their early years. Although for genetic or other reasons you might have a brain that is slightly better developed in some areas, it is not developed enough to produce something valued by society. Any area in which you engage in Virtuous Practice will develop that aspect of your brain, and hence those capacities.

In this light, giftedness is not something bestowed on a lucky few. Every individual has the capacity to change their brain and develop new abilities. If a few individuals have a slight head start, that does not impart upon them a long-term advantage, and it does not deny anyone else the ability to build a brain capable of much more.

The Rule of Practice holds because working within your Comfort and Performance Zones simply utilises existing neural pathways. It might make those pathways more reliable, but it can't produce new abilities. New abilities come from changing the way your brain works, which occurs through re-wiring your brain. This only happens as you push beyond your Comfort Zone, forcing your brain to find or create the connections that work best and strengthen them. The *virtue* of Virtuous Practice is that it creates a brain capable of doing things that it could not do before.

This is why, as explained in our Learning Agility diagram, we build potential when we apply our Growth Mindset to our Virtuous Practice. The real achievement of the expert performer is not their performance – it is the backstory of Virtuous Practice that created a brain capable of the expert performance; a brain with more potential than it had at the start of the journey. Their performance is simply evidence of this achievement.

The Rule of Effort holds because the development of new talents requires the development of new behaviours. These behaviours are governed by the way the brain is wired and hence subject to improvement through the process of Virtuous Practice. Once we have developed these new neural pathways, we can apply them to becoming even more effective at how we engage in Virtuous Practice.

Section 3.4: The Rule of Unlimited Growth

For example, as we develop our ability to think creatively, we improve our capacity for finding solutions to novel problems. Likewise, our capacity to think interdependently helps us become more effective at engaging in Virtuous Practice by drawing on the knowledge of others.

Finally, the Rule of Unlimited Potential holds because, to the best of our knowledge, there is no point at which your brain is no longer able to rewire itself and create new abilities. There are certainly times during a person's life when the brain appears to be more plastic than others, but at no point does it become static and incapable of improving talents and abilities.

The underlying reality that governs the Rule of Practice is that the brain can change. If our brains were not capable of change, then the worldview of the Fixed Mindset would be true. The abilities you were born with, whether you had immediate access to them, or had to "tap into them", would be what you had for life. Your potential would be limited, and some people would be better than others simply by virtue of the brain they were born with. Fortunately, this is not the case, and it turns out that most people's inability to grow and improve is the result of not knowing how to go about building their talents.

Now that we have a deep understanding of the Four Rules About Talent, we know that everyone is capable of significant growth. But the Four Rules do not mean that anyone can be anything, and they certainly don't mean that anyone can become rich and/or famous. All they mean is that everyone can improve, and that there's no limit to that improvement.

We will explore why you may not be able to be anything you want in the next section.

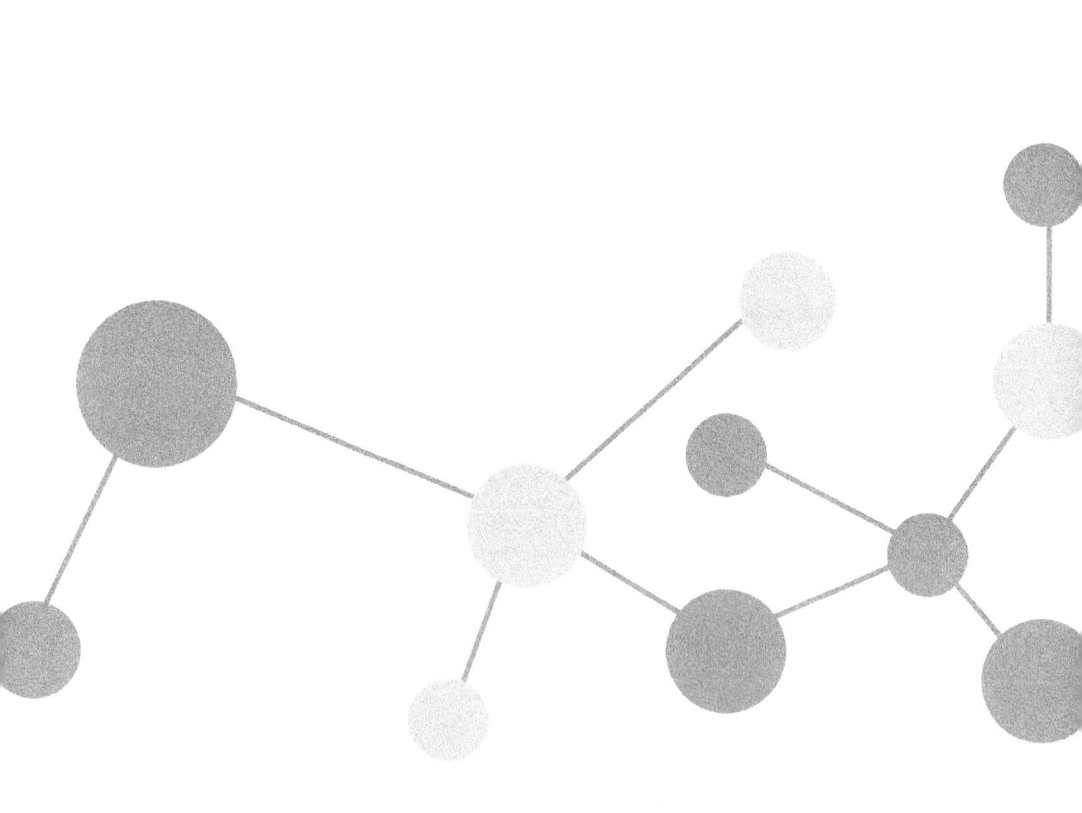

SECTION 4
New Ideas About Talent

SECTION 4
New Ideas About Talent

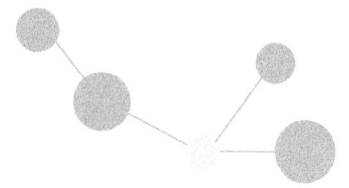

What's Possible?

As we become familiar with the Four Rules About Talent, it's easy to start thinking that we can achieve anything we want. We have choice; practice and effort will always result in growth; and, by virtue of the fact our brain is capable of rewiring itself, growth is unlimited. Given these truths, why couldn't anyone achieve anything? Or, for that matter, why can't we achieve everything?

The only promise made by the Four Rules About Talent is that we are capable of growth. Recall that in Section 1 we spoke about success. The definition we used for success was about improvement and mastery. It was about changing ourselves and being better than we were yesterday. Success, we defined, was about personal growth, and being able to change your most basic characteristics – including your talents, abilities and intelligence. The Four Rules About Talent tell us there's nothing about who you are that stops you taking that next step in your growth.

This, of course, does not mean we can achieve everything. Apart from the influence of circumstance and opportunity, growth takes time. Whether it's 10 000 hours, as author Malcolm Gladwell has suggested, or some other amount, it's certainly a long time. No-one becomes exceptionally good at anything without many hours of practice. We simply don't live long enough to get good at everything, so we need to make choices about where we are to spend our time and energy.

There are many other factors that affect whether we'll achieve our goals. If our goals are internal – that is, they are about ourselves and developing our abilities – then the Four Rules About Talent will help us achieve them. However, being able to grow is not the same as achieving a certain amount of growth. The amount of growth we experience may be influenced by circumstances, opportunity and even sheer luck.

At other times, we may set ourselves goals that are external, such as achieving a position or role, or being better than someone else. Sometimes our goals may involve fame or fortune. None of these are promised by the Four Rules About Talent.

Those who have reached the peak of their fields have followed the Four Rules About Talent. Often, the Four Rules and the development of Learning Agility do lead to people achieving external goals, such as awards, promotions and even fame and fortune, but it's worth spending some time exploring the roles other factors play.

Circumstance and Opportunity

Circumstance and opportunity matter. To follow the Four Rules About Talent, you must have the opportunity to engage in Virtuous, and preferably Deliberate, Practice. Unfortunately, not everyone has that opportunity.

A person's financial situation can certainly contribute to their capacity to engage in Virtuous Practice. Everyone has the capacity to develop their ability in music, but if your parents can't afford to give you music lessons and therefore you're denied the opportunity to practice, then it's unlikely you will become a great musician.

Where you live can matter in the most unexpected ways. In his wonderful book *Bounce: Mozart, Federer, Picasso, Beckham, and the Science of Success (Harper Perennial, 2011)*, Matthew Syed tells his story of being an elite table tennis player. He points out that Silverdale Road, England – his home at the time – produced more outstanding table tennis players than the rest of the country in the 1980s. It turns out that living in this location gave people an advantage, because it was near the Omega Club that allowed players to train 24 hours a day, and also happened to be home to one of the best coaches available at the time. So, if you didn't live near Silverdale Road and wanted to be an elite table tennis player, you would have been at a disadvantage.

It's not just where you are born that can make a difference, but when you are born can also play a critical role. It turns out that being born in the first three months of the year gives junior hockey players in Canada a distinct advantage in becoming an elite hockey player,

The reason is stunning. The cut-off date for an age group is 31 December. The result is that children playing in the same age group who were born in the first few months of the year are almost one year older than the players born in the last few months of the year. Because these January to March children are a bit bigger, their maturity gets mistaken for talent, and they are more likely to be selected for the "A" League. These squads train more often, and under the direction of better coaches, so these children can engage in more practice, thus becoming better hockey players! The result is that 40% of players in any elite squad in Canada will have been born between January and March.

Of course, other factors play a role. Not everyone who's born in the first three months of the year will make it to the elite level. You've also got to have the right body size (as an adult), live close enough to an ice hockey facility to train, and have parents who can afford to pay training fees and are prepared to take you to training. Circumstance and opportunity matter, but when all other factors are equal, only those who have the advantage of more practice are the ones who become elite.

Innate Ability and Selection Bias

Ericsson and Pool (2016) discusses the impact of innate ability on future performance. While adult-level performance is purely the result of Virtuous Practice, it is possible to stand out from your peers in the early years based on innate ability. In a similar way that slightly older, physically larger children are selected for representative squads and receive extra practice, early natural ability can give you opportunities others miss out on.

Ericsson describes how this effect could happen in chess. Chess requires good spatial awareness – the same characteristic developed by the London taxi drivers discussed earlier. Spatial awareness is measured by IQ tests, which means that children with higher IQs tend to have an easier time learning the early moves in chess. You can imagine how this early "ability" might lead to these students being selected for further training – and, as a result, they would continue to get better. Those without the "natural" ability would be less likely to be selected for further training, so they do not get better.

However, we know that when it comes to adult-level performance, excellence in chess is the result of the accumulation of many hours of Deliberate Practice. The best grandmaster chess champions are not necessarily those with the highest IQs, but only those with reasonably high IQs were given the opportunity to practice in the first place. So, we can unfairly bias the sample when we make selections based on "innate" ability. As Ericsson points out, it is notoriously difficult to predict future performance based on a current standard. The reason, of course, being that your future performance has little to do with who you are, and lots to do with what you do.

Ericsson refers to this sort of selection bias as the "dark side of natural ability". How often is a person given the opportunity to further develop their talents and abilities because of a slight advantage? Given that on an adult scale your talents and abilities are the result of Virtuous Practice, how many people have been denied the opportunity to engage in that practice because they lacked early "natural" ability?

Success and Sport

In any discussion about success and talent, someone is going to bring up a sporting example. "Surely," they'll say, "not everyone can be a great athlete. Look at those basketball players, they're all seven feet tall. No way I'm ever going to be an NBL star at five foot six!" And they'd be right! The Four Rules About Talent do not guarantee you a place in an elite sporting team, no matter how much you practice.

When we talk about sporting examples, we encounter two fundamental problems. First, that we've changed our definition of success. In sports, success is about being better than someone else, but in this book, success is about being better than yourself. You can always improve your own abilities (given the opportunity to engage in Virtuous Practice), but that does not necessarily mean you'll come to be better than someone else, especially when there are other factors at play, such as body size.

The second problem is that there are real fixed traits that give you a distinct advantage in some sports. No matter how hard you train, you can't learn to be taller! You could engage in hours of Virtuous Practice and become the most skilful basketball player in the world, but if you're only five feet tall, the reality of the way the game is played means that the less skilled, but much taller player, will likely get a place on the team instead of you.

It is important to recognise, though, that success in sports is still largely due to Virtuous Practice. Players who get to the top tend to have both the physical characteristics and to have done the practice.

You can think about these fixed physical characteristics in the same way we've spoken about other opportunities. Having the physical characteristics advantageous for a sport gives you an opportunity to become elite in that sport – an opportunity denied to someone who lacks those characteristics. But you must still take advantage of that opportunity and do the required hours of Virtuous Practice to become great. There are plenty of people out there with the desired physical characteristics for a particular sport, but they have not done the practice to build their skills. This reflects the Rule of Choice: you can choose where to develop your skills.

Fame and Fortune

The Four Rules About Talent do not offer you fame and fortune, either, but they can certainly help you achieve them.

Fame and fortune are external goals. The Four Rules About Talent work on building your talent and abilities. Unfortunately, fame and fortune are not always the reward for the person with the most talent.

To make money from your abilities, they must be applied to something society wants. The *Guinness World Records* books are full of people who have developed talents and abilities society finds interesting, but won't pay a lot of money to see. For example, you might be the most talented plate spinner in the world, but my guess is that it's unlikely to make you lots of money, or fill a stadium with people wanting to watch you do it! Conversely, there are many people we might consider moderately talented who make a fortune. In professional basketball, for example, there are many players who make a good living from the sport who don't play anywhere near the same level as the top players.

Fame is a more difficult and fickle proposition. When we think of fame, we often think of areas such as the music industry. Success in the music industry does not necessarily go to the person who can sing or play their instrument the best. In *Outliers*, Gladwell points to The Beatles as examples of a successful band, crediting their success to the many hours of practice in their early days in Hamburg. But while this practice certainly helped, most people would agree that they weren't technically the best musicians at the time. A review of the Top 40 pop hits at any point in time quickly reveals that the most popular, successful or famous musicians are not necessarily the ones who are the most musically talented.

The Beatles' fame did not come solely from their technical skills as musicians. The song-writing partnership of Lennon and McCartney also played a major role, as did the work of the "fifth Beatle" – producer Sir George Martin. Further external factors played a role as well, such as their look and being the right age at the right time to appeal to the British market.

Fame is the result of what the community happens to value. This is not always the person with the most talent. Sometimes a person can achieve fame simply by being in the right place at the right time. And success isn't always about building talent in one narrow field. More often, it's about knowing which talents to build at a certain time. Investing in a good manager might be more important than investing more hours into learning to play the guitar. Commercial success may go to the person who knows which areas are "good enough", and which talents need further development.

The Road to Success Isn't Always Well-Defined

It's all well and good to talk about building talent in the areas typically studied by Ericsson and others: classical music, chess, table tennis and ice hockey. These are narrow fields with clearly defined standards of what it means to be successful and well-known paths to mastery – you must do A, then B, then C ... then X, Y and Z. And, of course, these characteristics make them easier areas to study.

But what about areas such as business, parenting, teaching or building a relationship with your partner? Many people we define as talented or successful in these areas are quite different. They haven't followed a common path, and although we might recognise two people as very good or successful, they're not the "same" good. The standards we use to judge success in these areas are much more diverse, and relate to achieving broad outcomes that can be reached in different ways, rather than specific, narrow outcomes achieved through a common process.

Most things we do in life are multifaceted, so it is not about who can build the greatest skill set, but who can build the right skill set to solve the problems in front of them. These problems are often situational, change regularly and differ from one person to the next.

Being successful in business is not about learning one skill, and then the next. Instead, it is about recognising which aspect of your skill set you need to develop next. This will be different for different people, and even getting to the "top" in business doesn't necessarily mean you've accumulated the same set of skills as another industry leader. It simply means that you've accumulated the talents and abilities required for your business success.

The same is true for parenting, relationships, teaching and any number of real-life situations – that's why this book is about Learning Agility, and not just Virtuous Practice. If life was simply about deciding what you wanted to do, then setting out to develop a well-defined skill set to perform specific, narrow tasks, then Deliberate Practice would be king. But most of life is not like that. Life doesn't present us with the goal of developing a prescribed set of abilities, it presents us with the necessity to develop the required set of abilities to face unpredictable challenges.

Learning Agility allows us to develop the talents and abilities necessary to respond to the increasingly unpredictable challenges we face in life. Learning Agility gives us the understanding that we are capable of growth: our Growth Mindset. It also gives us the knowledge of how to go about achieving growth: through powerful Habits of Mind and Virtuous Practice. Being able to successfully face increasingly difficult challenges allows us to develop our abilities, which, in turn, means we can often achieve success in the areas we choose to pursue.

We can admire people for their success in a single area – the great sports star, the accomplished violinist – but sometimes they are what I'd call "long and skinny" successful. All their time and effort has been spent pursuing a single goal, sometimes at the expense of other areas of their lives.

More often though, we admire and aspire to be the person with a more rounded type of success. Those who have been able to grow in their careers, their relationships, their contributions to the community and their understanding of themselves. They may not be "the best", but they've always grown and improved where they needed to.

We admire these people's ability to respond to diverse challenges in different aspects of their lives. For most of us, this is what success is all about: responding to and overcoming the challenges we face at the time. This is what Learning Agility gives you. This is what this book is all about.

The Choice Not to Grow

"But what if I just want to spend my life sitting on the beach?" What if someone doesn't want to spend all that time and hard work improving? Isn't that a valid a form of success? My answer to this is always a qualified, "It depends."

It depends on whether or not it's a real choice. A Growth Mindset is the understanding that you're capable of growth, but it does not mean you're *obliged* to grow. I have a strong Growth-Oriented Mindset about my ability to play music. I understand that with time and resources, I could become an accomplished musician, but I choose not to do that. I don't want to spend time and energy improving my musical abilities, so I spend my time and energy in other areas instead. I pursue the goals I've set myself in life.

When I hear people use the "but what if I don't want to improve" argument, my question is always, "Is that a real choice?" Is that person choosing to spend their life sitting on the beach because they truly don't want anything else, even though they understand that they are capable of improving? Or is it because they don't believe that they can improve? Is saying, "I don't want to", a defence mechanism for their Fixed Mindset? Perhaps what they're really saying is, "If I tried, I think I'd fail. And I'd rather tell people I don't want to, than to try and fail."

Humans have free will, meaning that we can choose how we want to spend our lives, and we can set our own goals. Further, the Rule of Choice tells us that we are capable of growth in any area we choose. So, if you want to spend your life sitting on the beach, or if you don't want to get better at your job, or you don't want to improve your relationship, you're free to choose that. But I would argue that you can't call it "your choice" if you believed there was no alternative.

I'm not talking about not choosing to engage in the rat race, or getting caught up in other people's goals. What I'm talking about is whether you choose to rise to the challenges in your life.

Recall that the Growth Mindset is about choice. The Fixed Mindset and the Greatness Gap take away that choice. They tell you that you can't change, and that you must work out where you fit in the world and get used to your lot in life. Further, because you can't change who you are, all you're left with is to change people's perception of you: who they think you are. My feeling is that the "but what if all I want is ... " argument is often a way of protecting the identity created by a Fixed Mindset.

> There's a big difference between not getting better at something because you don't want to, and not getting better because you don't believe you can.

All this raises the interesting question: What motivates us to make these choices?

What About Motivation?

Recall the Greatness Gap. To someone with a Fixed Mindset, the Greatness Gap exists because they believe some people are born different – born with natural talent. Throughout this book, I've made the case that these people weren't born different, rather they've just *done* something different. The Four Rules About Talent explain how we are all capable of significant growth in any area we choose.

The people we instinctively recognise as successful have spent their lives constantly responding to challenges. They have applied Effective Effort. They have built Learning Power. Their backstory is one of building themselves a better brain so they can accomplish their goals. They may have even spent their entire life developing their abilities in one narrow field.

In light of this backstory of consistent, hard work, it's easy to imagine that the difference between the people we consider successful and ourselves is not the *ability* to get better, but the *desire*! The greatness Greatness Gap is not about talent or ability, it's about motivation!

What motivates these people to work so hard? It's a valid question to ask, and it's tempting to believe that these people love doing hard work. They weren't born with their level of ability, so maybe they were born with a motivation and drive that led them to work harder than others? But this isn't true.

There are two important aspects of the motivation side of this story. The first is that the best don't love hard work more than anyone else. Studies by Ericsson (2016) into what motivates the best to work so hard found that it's not that these people love hard work, they simply understand that it is necessary to improve performance. They understand the Four Rules About Talent and recognise that hard work is essential. That's it. They work hard not because they love to practice, but because they love to improve. So, the question then becomes: what motivates them to love to improve?

Unfortunately, research into where we get our motivations from doesn't give us a clear answer. In his book, *Drive: The Surprising Truth About What Motivates Us* (Riverhead Books, 2009), Daniel Pink does a wonderful job of capturing our current understanding of what motivates people. Among other factors, he points out that we aren't born with motivation – we catch it.

Most people go through their younger years not knowing how they want to spend their lives. Walk into any school and start talking to students about their future, and you will find that very few have an overriding motivation to pursue a particular goal. But talk to people who are later in life, and many more will have "found" their passion.

As Pink points out, at some point in their lives, the best catch their motivation. The sources of this motivation vary enormously. Some are motivated by a passionate individual who "lights their fire" – a parent, teacher or mentor. Others refer to an inspirational moment, something they saw or experienced. Others report that they were motivated by love, or even spite. What's clear is that they all initially "catch" their motivation from something external, and this is where Mindset plays a critical role.

> Perhaps the single greatest reason we need to be working with students' Mindsets is motivation.

I worry about the number of children who cruise through school, unsure of what they want to do with their lives or unclear about their passions. Children who, at some point in time, will connect with that external spark that could ignite that drive, a motivation that could set their life's course. I worry about the number of students who will reach that moment, struck by wonderment and awe, where the spark that lights their passion hits its mark. And then, hot on the heels of their excitement, comes the thought, "But I'm not like them." Instead of passionately pursing something that might become their life's goal, they create the Greatness Gap, which extinguishes the spark. They become interested bystanders, instead of passionately pursuing what might become their life's goal.

At the heart of the Growth Mindset is the understanding that you're capable of pursing your goals and passions. Learning Agility fuels your motivation by giving you an understanding of the pathway you can follow to get from where you are now to where you want to be. It gives you an understanding that you can build your backstory. Learning Agility does not motivate you – it breathes life into your motivation, leading you to take action to pursue your goals.

Hard Work and Backstory

As Pablo Picasso said, "Action is the foundational key to all success." To grow, and to improve your abilities, you must do the hard work. This work extends over a long period of time, and it is only as we do it that we improve. Your backstory is one of long periods of hard work that create increases in your abilities and improvements in your performance.

It's tempting to look at someone's life story and focus on the end point: their highest accomplishments or their greatest talents. Considering where they ended up, it's easy to see their earlier, lesser accomplishments as being "obvious". "Of course," we say, "Steve Jobs could run a start-up company out of his garage. He ended up running one of the most successful companies on the planet. A small start-up out of the garage would be *easy* for him." But this belief is mistaken. At the time Jobs started Apple, he wasn't destined to be great. Before he could *be* great, he had to *become* great by building his own backstory. Taking that first step, and every step after it, is hard work!

Yes, I imagine that today, were he still alive, Steve Jobs would find running a small business out of his garage easy. But we must remember that everything is hard before it is easy. Jobs grew as a result of his experiences, and what was once hard for him became easy because he learnt to behave more intelligently. Jobs wasn't smart enough to create and run Apple when he was in his early 20s – he was only smart enough to run a small business in his garage … until he got smarter!

We make a fundamental mistake when we judge a person's early work by their current, peak performance. What we must recognise is that at every step in their backstory, they were working at their best, their peak performance. They were literally incapable, at that point in time, of doing any better. To do better, they had to become better. They had to build a backstory, and to do that they developed Learning Agility.

The Final Word: Learning Agility

Being an Agile Learner involves understanding that we are capable of growth, and that we are not born with our abilities, but develop them throughout our lives. As Ericsson and Pool (2016) put it, "Talent is not the cause of something, but the result. It does not create a process, it is the end result of that process." Our understanding of this is our Growth Mindset.

Section 4: New Ideas About Talent

To maintain our Growth Mindset, we must be alert to the negative Mindset Movers around us. These are the messages that break the Four Rules About Talent, and suggest to us that we are limited. This is especially important for teachers and parents as we nurture the development of a Growth Mindset in our children as, ultimately, it will be a Growth Mindset that opens doors for them to pursue their dreams.

A Growth Mindset also gives you the understanding that when life throws unexpected challenges at you, you are capable of successfully responding to them. This is critical for children today, who are growing up in a world that is increasingly unpredictable and changing. Perhaps there was a time in the not-so-distant past when it was possible for most people to follow well-worn paths, doing what others had done before them, but that is no longer the case. The challenges that confront children in schools today are often novel and complex.

> But a Growth Mindset is not growth, it is just the understanding that you can grow. It forms the foundation for Learning Agility because it invites you to engage in actions that will lead to growth. But if those actions aren't the right sort of actions, then you will fail to grow.

Because the problems facing us today are not only new – they are also more difficult, complex and demanding – we need to learn to behave more intelligently than in the past. Solving increasingly difficult problems requires us to learn to behave increasingly intelligently. This is where the work of Costa and Kallick, in describing the Habits of Mind, becomes so important. We must seek not only to use these "intelligent behaviours", but to use them better and, in doing so, develop Learning Power.

Learning Power is of little use to us if we do not apply it in the right way. To grow and develop new abilities, we must push ourselves beyond our current best and engage in Virtuous Practice. We need to engage in Ericsson's 3 Fs of Virtuous Practice: to *focus* on what we are trying to achieve, receive *feedback* on our progress (preferably from an expert, or at least a clear set of standards) and make adjustments based on this feedback to *fix it*.

Engaging in Virtuous Practice with Learning Power makes our efforts efficacious, leading to growth. Of course, underlying all of this is the deep reality behind the Growth Mindset: our brain's ability to rewire itself. Without this ability, our potential truly would be limited. Fortunately, our brains aren't limited by the way they are wired today. We build our potential through engaging in Virtuous Practice and building ourselves a better brain, one that is capable of doing things that were not previously possible.

There is a great message of hope in Learning Agility. It does not promise that we can be or do anything – circumstance and opportunity play a role – but when we understand the Four Rules About Talent, we understand that there is nothing about who we are that stops us from improving. We are always capable of further growth, and we are not limited by our nature, only our circumstances. Embedded in that is a huge social justice issue that we must address as a society.

In concluding this book, I'm reminded of the words of one of the world's pre-eminent educators, Benjamin Bloom (1985), who said:

> After 40 years of intensive research on school learning in the United States as well as abroad, my major conclusion is: What one person in the world can learn, almost all persons can learn, if provided with the appropriate prior and current conditions of learning.

As educators, it is our responsibility to provide those conditions for learning, and to develop the Learning Agility that allows learning to take place in an increasingly challenging and changing world!

SUGGESTED READINGS

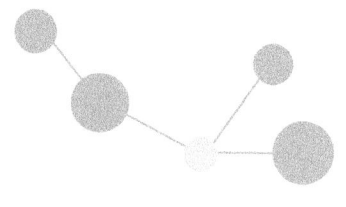

If you have found the ideas in *The Agile Learner* interesting, then you may also find insights and further learning in these titles. All of them have been a part of my learning journey, and have contributed in one way or another to the ideas expressed here.

Anderson, J. 2010. *Succeeding with Habits of Mind: Developing, Infusing and Sustaining the Habits of Mind for a More Thoughtful Classroom*. Melbourne, Victoria: Hawker Brownlow Education.

Bloom, B. S. 1985. *Developing Talent in Young People*. New York, NY: Ballantine Books.

Brienco, E. 2015. Mistakes Are Not All Created Equal. *Mindset Works' Blog*. Available at: http://blog.mindsetworks.com/entry/mistakes-are-not-all-created-equal [Accessed 25 October 2017]

Colvin, G. 2010. *Talent is Overrated: What Really Separates World-Class Performers from Everybody Else*. New York, NY: Portfolio.

Costa, A. "The Search for Intelligent Life" in Costa, A. (Ed). 1985. *Developing Minds, Volume 1: A Resource Book for Teaching Thinking*. Alexandra, VA: ASCD.

Costa, Arthur L. & Kallick, B. (Ed's). 2008. *Learning and Leading with Habits of Mind: 16 Essential Characteristics for Success*. Alexandria, VA: ASCD.

Costa, Arthur L. & Kallick, B. 2014. *Dispositions: Reframing Teaching and Learning*. Thousand Oaks, CA: Corwin.

Coyle, D. 2009. *The Talent Code: Greatness Isn't Born. It's Grown. Here's How*. New York, NY: Bantam Books.

Doidge, N. 2010. *The Brain that Changes Itself: Stories of Personal Triumph from the Frontiers of Brain Science*. Carlton North, Victoria: Scribe Publications.

Dweck, C. S. 2006. *Mindset: The New Psychology of Success*. New York, NY: Random House.

Ericsson, K. A. 1996. *The Road to Excellence: The Acquisition of Expert Performance in the Arts and Sciences, Sports, and Games*. Mahwah, NJ: Lawrence Erlbaum Associates.

Ericsson, K. A. & Pool, R. 2016. *Peak: Secrets from the New Science of Expertise*. Boston, MA: Houghton Mifflin Harcourt.

Foer, J. 2011. *Moonwalking with Einstein: The Art and Science of Remembering Everything*. New York, NY: Penguin Books.

Gardner, H. 2011. *Frames of Mind: The Theory of Multiple Intelligences*, 3rd edition. New York, NY: Basic Books.

Gladwell, M. 2008. *Outliers: The Story of Success*. New York, NY: Little, Brown and Company.

Gross-Loh, C. 2016. How Praise Became a Consolation Prize: Helping Children Confront Challenges Requires a More Nuanced Understanding of the "Growth Mindset". *The Atlantic*. Available at: https://www.theatlantic.com/education/archive/2016/12/how-praise-became-a-consolation-prize/510845/ [Accessed 25 October 2017]

Howe, M. J. A. 1999. *Genius Explained*. Cambridge, UK: Cambridge University Press.

Kaufman, S. B. 2013. *Ungifted: Intelligence Redefined*. New York, NY: Basic Books.

Maguire, E. A., Woolett, K. & Spiers, H. J. 2006. London Taxi Drivers and Bus Drivers: A Structural MRI and Neuropsychological Analysis. *Hippocampus*, 16(12), pp. 1091–1101.

Sacks, O. 1985. *The Man Who Mistook His Wife for a Hat and Other Clinical Tales*. New York, NY: Summit Books.

Shank. D. 2011. *The Genius in All of Us: New Insights into Genetics, Talent and IQ*. New York, NY: Anchor.

Syed, M. 2011. *Bounce: Mozart, Federer, Picasso, Beckham, and the Science of Success*. New York, NY: Harper Perennial.

www.ingramcontent.com/pod-product-compliance
Lightning Source LLC
Chambersburg PA
CBHW062035290426
44109CB00026B/2634